W9-DED-119

Our Debt to Greece and Rome

EDITORS

GEORGE DEPUE HADZSITS, PH.D.

DAVID MOORE ROBINSON, PH.D., LL.D.

SENECA THE PHILOSOPHER
AND HIS MODERN MESSAGE

BY
RICHARD MOTT GUMMERE

COOPER SQUARE PUBLISHERS, INC.
NEW YORK
1963

Published 1963 by Cooper Square Publishers, Inc.
59 Fourth Avenue, New York 3, N. Y.
Library of Congress Catalog Card No. 63-10274

To

THE MEMORY OF MY FATHER

FRANCIS BARTON GUMMERE

*Vivit: ad posteros usque transiluit et se in
memoriam dedit.* (SENECA)

"He lives in life that ends not with his breath."

EDITORS' PREFACE

THE LIBRARY, " Our Debt to Greece and Rome," should reveal the inherited permanent factors in the civilization of the twentieth century which have resisted the effects of chance and time and outlived the ephemeral experiments of man. Those classifications of our intellectual, moral and spiritual life, which have had their origin in the Greek and Roman world and which have steadied human life and thinking ever since, are today of enormous importance for determining the aim and direction of life and for creating a sense of unity in life. These elements in our life are the bases of civilization, upon which the fancy and imagination of the human mind may build, but without which or without knowledge of which, life sails upon an uncharted sea. Whether in philosophy, science or religion, in literature or language, in art or architecture, or in political thinking we are so largely Greek and Roman, European and American civilizations are so shot through and through with the ancient traditions and habits of thought, that we can understand ourselves and our institutions only as we comprehend that large inherited element and the history of its influence. " We think in terms like those idiomatic in Rome and Greece." The Hebraic mood and mind, alone, of the ancient past, possess a hold comparable to that of Greece and Rome upon our thinking and imagination. Greece has been the source of most of our aspirations, and Rome, the great mediator.

An account of the long-continued Influence of these ancient forces, the vicissitudes of their acceptance, of correct or of false application or even of rejection, possess a peculiar charm and fascination. This Library will furnish a fresh appraisal of these Influences and will point out the values of ancient forms as a constant guidance to human endeavor, as a constant corrective in the midst of crises, as a constant inspiration for a better world. It is this aspect of human history that will engage the writers of the volumes in this Series, who may thereby contribute much, not merely to a better understanding of this historical phenomenon, but also to a true recognition of the

supreme importance to civilization of those elements of the ancient world that are deathless.

A clear exposition, therefore, of those inherited elements, of their survival through medieval Europe, of their effects upon the Renaissance, upon later European and American civilization, of their influence today, should lead to
a clearer understanding of ourselves, which is
the first essential for true progress. To what
extent that legacy will possess value for the
future, time alone will tell. Far from advo-
cating stereotyped thinking according to traditional forms, which we must constantly revise,
we should at least as individuals, as a society,
as a civilization, know ourselves in order to
establish a firm foundation for a new specula-
tion and for a new freedom, in order to attain
an independence that is truly rational. If from
the past some traditions have come that serve
as unworthy inhibitions, we shall come to know
their unworthiness only by a study of their
historic development. On the other hand, we
predict a clear revelation, through the pages of
this new Series, of many *abiding values,* whose
merit is determined not merely by fancied
vested rights existing in tradition, but established by reason of inherent worth and trial.

It is the hope of the Editors that these eternal principles that have animated and actuated life so long will stand out more clearly by reason of the books of this Library, and that, in consequence, the riddle of the Sphinx, which is the riddle of existence, will seem a little less forbidding.

The volume on Seneca by Doctor Gummere is the first to appear in the Series, known as " Our Debt to Greece and Rome."

The volume represents an effort to explain, as far as may be possible within the limits of a small volume, the nature and extent of the influence of the philosophy of Seneca, which has been of perennial interest and importance through the ages following the life, work and death of the great Roman philosopher and statesman of the empire.

That such an influence has persisted is of sufficient interest to mark the philosophy of Seneca as one of broad character and of vital content. For systems rise and fall, men come and go, and the whims of Time pay little heed to the irrelevant and the insignificant.

The reader will discover the underlying reasons for the continued appeal of Seneca's message and mission to the Europe of later date, not to mention a still further sweep of that religious and ethical system into the thought, life and literature of another people across the seas. That Seneca still lives, that the modernity of Seneca is characteristic of a mind transcending the limits of time and space, that Seneca will continue to mold human aspirations, these are some of the inevitable conclusions from a reading of the essay that follows.

CONTENTS

[xiii]

PREFACE

L UCIUS ANNAEUS SENECA, the prime
minister of Nero, the outstanding figure
of his age, and the author of many
political and philosophical experiments, was far
ahead of his contemporaries. That is the chief
reason for the very downright opinions, *pro*
and *con*, which have been expressed during
nineteen centuries regarding his personality and
his works. However varyingly the world has
rated him, the last two decades have brought
him into his own. Instead of a gossip-laden
courtier, Seneca has been proved a constructive
statesman; instead of a second-hand philosopher, he has come to be viewed as the Bossuet
of Imperial Rome, lacking the simplicity of
Musonius and Epictetus, but handling his contemporaries without gloves and advising them
as the French bishop advised the circle of
Louis XIV. There is no doubt that fuller investigation reveals him as a man of originality,
vitality and power.

It is this disregard of crusted tradition that
any unbiased student of Seneca's writings will

note with interest. The inner light of the Spirit, the sacred freedom of the individual, the greater respect due to women, the disapproval of slavery and gladiatorial combats, the work-ability of philosophy, the need of bringing personal standards into public life,— all these *motifs,* taken together, form a system of living which marks an advance over his ancient pre-decessors and contemporaries. He is, without doubt, one of the world's wise men, as Emerson testifies: " Make your own Bible. Select and collect all the words and sentences that in all your reading have been to you like the blast of triumph out of Shakespeare, Seneca, Moses, John and Paul."

It is accordingly the aim of this brief study to show how extensive has been the influence of his style, his thought, his experiment in philosopher-kingship, and the essential spiritu-ality of his message.

SENECA THE PHILOSOPHER
AND HIS MODERN MESSAGE

SENECA THE PHILOSOPHER AND HIS MODERN MESSAGE

I. THE OLD AND THE NEW

THE ROMAN of the Republic was a pragmatist. His interests were centred upon money, farming, engineering, law, oratory, and government. His literature was not original, and his mind was not speculative. Even his religion was as distinctly formulated as the other elements in his life; and with regard to philosophy, Ennius had warned him, in the second century B.C., " to bathe, but not to wallow in it."

When he grew rich, after the downfall of Carthage, he had cosmopolitanism and imperialism thrust upon him. He had some leisure. He bought bronzes, or laid out fancy gardens, or listened furtively to the novelties of Greek philosophy. Such a man would not be carried away by a creed of mystic aloofness. He would be interested in a system that combined theory with practice. And of all the Greek schools of thought he was most attracted by Stoicism.

This was the " world-citizen " creed which believed knowledge to be attainable and defined virtue as something different from the *laissez-faire* watchword of Epicureanism. It held to a regular sequence of sensation, mind-picture, concept, and knowledge. Stoicism bade the wise man master the science of government and the arts of speaking and writing. And furthermore, it promised a glimpse of immortality. All the other creeds of Greece were represented in Rome, but, as the Republic ended and the Empire began, Stoicism was the acknowledged leader.

Finally, in the period following Augustus, from 14 A.D. for many years, Stoicism became more than an aid to affairs; it grew into a spiritual prop. When public discussion was muzzled, when the Senate was a figurehead and the government a bureaucracy, this school of thought betook itself into the lecture-hall, the salon, and the home as a remedy and a comfort. Epicureans were indifferent; Academics met the situation by falling back upon learned doubt; Stoicism, however, began a line of thinkers which terminated with Marcus Aurelius but included, besides the well-known leaders, many an unheralded experimenter in spiritual endurance, physical courage, or mental defiance. There was no creed that more closely resembled the coming Christianity than this Eastern-born gospel of clear-thinking patience.

As philosophy proceeded from a plaything to a creed, so government, by the time of the Emperors, had changed from a by-product to a profession. Before the Punic wars there were thousands of Latin freeholders who took part in politics as a matter of course and divided up the duties of the state. We read of aristocratic governing classes and plebeian " consenters," each with its own machinery of expression, trending through compromise to union. The situation was like that in England during the nineteenth century, when one Reform Bill after another brought the people to comparative uniformity. Under the Empire, however, the expert was everything, and the citizen in general a pawn. The whole world had poured into Rome. Wandering threads had to be drawn together. Political action was in the hands of a few. Consequently, thought had no practical outlet. A Corbulo could be sent to the East; a Sejanus could tyrannize at Rome.

But it was all under the patronage and aegis of empire. In such an era the philosophy of government would be speculatively and theoretically bold; but it could not function unless it was assimilated by the agencies of government. Hence came at periodic intervals insurrection by groups and revolt by individuals.

As with thought and statecraft, so with style. The Latin language was born in simplicity and nursed in facts. It recorded triumphs, recited chants, or argued cases. Its wit was homely and its frills were all Greek. Cato is brief and sinewy. Plautus is as homely and Roman as his Greek models allow him to be. Except for satire, the types of literature are mostly imported for the sake of cultural apprenticeship among a people who must imitate before they begin to create. As the world, however, pours into Italy, poets put on literary plumage and become half original; orators study Athenian models until they rival their forbears, and Rhetoric enters upon the stage. After the masterpieces of the Golden Age and the muzzling of political expression, it was hard to say anything new; therefore one must say something striking. Oratory leaves the law-courts for the lecture-hall, poetry refines upon subtleties, and the Roman essay, or popular diatribe, becomes fashionable.

The world was thus ready for an interpreter, in new and striking terms, of this Silver Age cosmopolitanism. And it found such an interpreter in the person of Seneca the Younger, an innovator in philosophy, politics, and literature.

Seneca, whose personality has always been somewhat of a puzzle, was born about 4 B.C. in that mysterious land which was known to the Romans as a nurse of hardy and artistic tribesmen who for two hundred years, until the age of Augustus, had resisted the resources of Rome with more success than the volatile Gauls or the versatile Greeks.

" As *some grave Tyrian trader, from the sea,*
Descried at sunrise an emerging prow,
And saw the merry Grecian coaster come,
Freighted with amber grapes, and Chian wine,
Green bursting figs, and tunnies steeped in brine,
And knew the intruders on his ancient home,—

The young light-hearted masters of the waves,—
And snatched his rudder, and shook out more sail;
And day and night held on indignantly

[7]

O'er the blue Midland waters with the gale,
Betwixt the Syrtes and soft Sicily,
To where the Atlantic raves
Outside the western straits; and unbent sails
There, where down cloudy cliffs, through sheets
of foam,
Shy traffickers, the dark Iberians come;
And on the beach undid his corded bales."

Arnold, in his "Scholar-Gypsy," has pictured the scene well: trading Carthaginians, energetic but unstable Greeks, and strange natives.

Spain's early memorials are as elusive as her early history: the curious bust of the Lady of Elche, the wall-decorations of prehistoric man, certain ritual-survivals, coins stamped with horsemen and battle scenes,— all these serve to show that the Romans were dealing with no common folk. Their clan-characteristics are not clearly defined, nor is their individuality capable of classification, as is that of other provincial peoples in the Empire. Like the Emperor Hadrian and Seneca himself, they were sensitive, imaginative, shrewd and interesting. This may have been because they were not racially and politically homogeneous, or because of their Iberian strain, or because of later Celtic intermixtures. In the center of this peninsula, however, lay the Turdetani who inhabited Baetica (the modern Andalusia) and whose capital was Corduba, the birthplace of Seneca. They had the highest degree of civilization in the whole province, and yet they cannot be identified with certainty as either Celtic or Iberian.

For over a hundred years the course of empire had taken its way westward until, in the days of empire proper, Spain became a fixture in the Roman provincial system. Men of the Marco Polo type had travelled thither, advertising the charms of Cadiz or the fertile Lusitania (now Portugal) " where flowers bloom through nine months of the year, a bushel of wheat costs nine obols, a sheep two drachmae, and a plough-ox ten." The myths of Hercules and Geryon, of Ulysses and the town of Olisipo (Lisbon) which report claimed that he had founded, are early echoes of this romantic interest. The Spanish skipper, with his heart full of gallantry and his pockets full of gold, is familiar to us from the Odes of Horace; [1] and the clever Balbus, a native Spaniard and agent of Julius Caesar, is an epitome of this progressive nation. In addition to all

[9]

his business ventures, Balbus wrote a historical drama entitled *Iter,*— an account of his mission to Pompey in 49 B.C. Business and romance went hand in hand. Mines, vineyards, olive-groves, and esparto grass were to make the fortune of many a Roman.

Corduba (now Cordova) was founded as early as 150 B.C. It earned the right to be the capital of a senatorial province, and grew into a political and literary centre, especially famous for schools of rhetoric as well as for its alle-giance to the Republican tradition of Pompey. Caesar never forgave this, but Augustus toler-ated and utilized it for the purpose of solidify-ing his conquests among the wilder tribes of the north and west. From this city sprang

> " *The learned Seneca's house*
> *That is thrice to be numbered.*" [2]

Lucius Annaeus Seneca the Elder, father of the philosopher whom this book discusses, was a manager of provincial finances, a *procurator* of the Imperial government, whose connections were of the best equestrian, or knightly, tradi-tions and whose salary may have reached 300,000 sesterces ($15,000). We do not know whether he was an importation from Rome, or

[10]

descended from early Roman settlers, or born of an intelligent native family. His title to fame is a book of rhetorical memoirs, dedicated to his three sons, although he himself would doubtless prefer to be remembered as an administrator rather than as an Isaac D'Israeli or a scissors-and-paste collector of oratorical anecdotes. He was a strict conservative, unlike his more distinguished son; he modelled his style upon Cicero, hated philosophy and all the strange cults which knocked at the gates of the Empire, and brought up his family like a Roman of the old school. His wife Helvia remains in the background; but her influence upon the younger Seneca was profound, and he dedicated to her one of the noblest tributes from a son to a mother in literary history. She was content to refrain from the mad rush of social Rome, and preferred to be the devoted mother of Gallio, the governor of Achaia, whose dealings with St. Paul we remember from the New Testament, of Lucius Annaeus the philosopher, and of Mela (father of the poet Lucan), who chose to follow his father's profession and amass a fortune through the usual Roman official channels. She outlived her husband and died about 39 A.D.

Such were the antecedents of Seneca; they assist us in our attempt to account for his blend of the millionaire and ascetic, for his literary catholicism, and for his attainment of the highest place in Rome short of the throne by means of his eloquence and his Stoicism. With such a background, it is not surprising that he appealed to Rousseau as a humanitarian, to Calvin as a guide for princes, and to Christians as a literary champion of new ideals.

About the beginning of the Christian era the sons of the elder Seneca were brought to Rome to be educated for government and administration. They had distinct advantages: they were free from the tarnished glamour of senatorial rank, and yet possessed of a wealthy and respectable inheritance. Lucius began his training under the care of a devoted aunt, wife of the governor of Egypt, a woman of such dignity that even the loose gossip of Alexandria held its tongue in her honour. As he grew older he visited there extensively; for the uncle was retained in his office for sixteen years by Tiberius, on the principle that a consistent policy was necessary in a part of the Empire that formed a critical and vital aid to the grain supply of Rome. His aunt nursed him through a dangerous illness, and later returned to Italy with the ashes of her husband, who had presumably died in office. The observations made by Lucius on the subject of death and its proper defiance are thus more than mere Stoic commonplaces. Such visits deepened his practical experience also. He learned at first hand the provincial theory of government and the management of finances on a large scale. And in this period he produced a work on the geography and religion of Egypt, as well as a pamphlet on the peoples of India; for Alexandria, the connecting link between East and West, was the clearing-house of such researches. It is interesting to note that as he began with geography and natural history, so he ended with them, publishing many years later a scientific work which dwells with special emphasis upon the flow and the sources of the Nile.

Through all these early days Seneca struggled continuously with ill health. Introspective by nature, he became still more so for this reason. He tells us that he leaned towards Pythagorean mysticism and several of the strange contemporary Eastern cults, and that he was only induced to throw away his philosophic eccentricities at the request of his practical and matter-of-fact father, with whom he had many a friendly argument, and whose *Life* he composed presumably after the year 39 A.D.

He remarks naïvely, apropos of his chronic catarrh: " I often entertained the impulse of ending my life then and there, but the thought of my kind old father " (some fifty years older than himself) " kept me back. For I reflected, not how bravely I had the power to die, but how little power he had to bear bravely the loss of me." Again: " Someone has made a joke about the baldness of my head, the weakness of my eyes, the thinness of my legs, the shortness of my stature; what insult is there in telling me what everyone sees? " He was subject to asthma throughout his life. We have many accounts of his plain diet, his life-long teetotalism, his cold-water baths, and his daily " road-work " to overcome physical handicaps.

But his young manhood was a happy one. It was marked by genial discussions with his father on the vagaries of philosophy, by love of country life at the various villas which the family owned, congenial association with his brilliant and popular brother Gallio (to whom he dedicated several of his works), marriage and children,[3] and a triumphant progress in the courts of law.

It is to be assumed that Seneca fulfilled the usual administrative apprenticeship by holding a curatorship of the mint, or a secretarial position in the Department of Public Works, or a magistracy in one of the lesser courts. And then, with the backing of his aunt, he attained the quaestorship, an office under the treasury which was regarded as the first real step into political prominence. This is supposed to have taken place about 33 A.D. Tiberius seems to have been on good terms with the whole family, because of his attitude toward the governor of Egypt, and also by reason of the elder Seneca's earnest desire that his son should not incur that emperor's displeasure by following the foreign worships against which Tiberius legislated in the year 19 A.D. It is significant that in Seneca's writings Augustus and Tiberius are treated on the whole with respect, while Caligula and Claudius come in for hatred and ridicule. Of Nero — more, later. That is the puzzle.

This hatred of Caligula perhaps originated in the jealousy of the mad emperor, who attacked

Seneca after a brilliant oratorical effort, sneered
at his style, called it " sand without lime " and
" mere school declamation," and would have
put him to death along with many another
promising citizen had not one of the court ladies
diverted him by remarking that the young
lawyer's delicate constitution would of itself do
what the emperor wished to do. He may have
been thinking of this episode when he wrote
to his friend Lucilius many years later:
" Disease has often postponed death, and a
vision of dying has been many a man's sal-
vation."

Prosperity was thus escorting Seneca along
the highroad to distinction. Whether he en-
tered the Senate under Tiberius is doubtful; but
it is entirely possible that his quaestorship had
qualified him therefor immediately. At any
rate he began to take his place as the literary
leader of society and the spiritual adviser to a
cultivated group of social leaders. Before the
death of Caligula in 41 he had written an essay
of consolation to Marcia, the daughter of Cre-
mutius Cordus,— one of those heroes on the
opposition benches to whom Tacitus, the his-
torian, pays respectful homage. And about
the same time he had produced his famous

treatise *On Anger,* which may be assumed to have resulted from observation of this vice in the habits of the late emperor. Seneca, as a member of the circle to which the princesses of the royal house belonged, could paint a realistic portrait of the monster. But, ironically enough, with all this success under a prince who had hated him, he came to grief under the next emperor, Claudius, a scholarly and legal person with whom he would have been supposed to stand on a most congenial footing.

Claudius was a sort of Roman James the First. He was a man of encyclopaedic learning, of literary taste, and of much experience in jurisprudence, antiquities, art, history, and linguistics. It was the Empress Messalina, whose cruel and beautiful face now looks appropriately down in marble upon visitors to the Capitoline Museum, to whom Seneca's disgrace may be ascribed. She hated the sisters of the late Caligula and the penetrating intellect of Seneca, who had given them his sympathy. The reason given at court was a too great intimacy between the Princess Julia and the rising statesman, although the gossiping Suetonius declares that the charge was vague and that no opportunity of defence was given. The fact that thirty-five senators and three hundred knights were executed under Claudius is also a proof of frequent injustice.

At all events, the penalty was *relegatio,* or banishment, with ensuing confiscation of half a man's property. The destination was the barren island of Corsica, whitewashed by " Jemmy " Boswell [4] as " a most agreeable island situated in the Mediterranean," correctly sketched without exaggeration by Mérimée in *Colomba* as a shrub-grown land of sandy soil and romantic associations, and anathematized in Seneca's first Epigram:

" I*sland of dread, when summer's heats begin,*
  M*ore savage when the Dog-star shows his teeth!*
  S*pare thou the banished,— rather spare thou those*
  W*ithin the tomb; and let thy earth lie light*
  U*pon the ashes of the living dead!* "

Here he spent eight years, from his forty-fifth to his fifty-third. We are not enlightened with regard to the exile's activities. We only know that a mouldering mass of ruins is still called " Seneca's tower," and that in Corsica he composed the tragedies which furnished the material for much of French drama and so unmistakably developed the Elizabethan stage.

We note three epochs in his exile literature which can be clearly marked out: in the first he takes the attitude of heroic and philosophic resignation, with a work on *Providence*, addressed to his friend Lucilius; another of the same sort on *The Steadfastness of the Sage*, dedicated to Serenus; and an essay of consolation to his mother, Helvia, — manly in spite of its occasional egoism. The second stage is revealed in a cringing letter to the powerful Polybius, one of the Emperor's rich freedmen secretaries. The third is one of quiet despair, unrecorded in actual output but reflected in his later works. His moods therefore ran the gamut peculiar to the sensitive temperament of one who saw his ambitions destroyed and his opportunities annihilated.

We must remember, however, that the general public felt kindly disposed toward Seneca even through these days of exile. When Fortune, whom the philosopher so often scorns in his writings, had come to his assistance in the most unexpected way, his restoration to grace was a popular action. In the year 49, when Messalina was removed from the scene, and the youthful Domitius, son of Agrippina and later to be the Emperor Nero, was in need of a tutor, Seneca was welcomed back to Rome, honoured with public office, and given the privileges of such responsibility. Tacitus, as usual, says much in a few words: " Agrippina obtained withdrawal from exile for Annaeus Seneca, and at the same time got him the praetorship, thinking that it would be a popular choice for two reasons, because of his reputation as a writer and for the sake of having her fledgling son grow up under such a training." So the barren Corsica was left behind, to appear before his eyes in the future only as a mirage or a memory, and he returned to the honours and the dangers of the imperial city. Several of his friends had been especially loyal to him: Annaeus Serenus, to whom were dedicated the essays *On Steadfastness, On Leisure,* and *On Peace of Mind;* Caesonius Maximus, in whose company it is likely he was dining when the centurion brought him the fateful message in the year 65; and Lucilius, his close companion and regular correspondent, to whom we owe the existence of the *Epistles* and the work *On Providence* and the *Natural History.* Gallio, with whom he conducted an extensive correspondence that was preserved after his death, and to whom he dedicated the essay *On the Happy Life,* never forsook him, nor did many of his friends, to whom he collectively utters frequent words of appreciation. It is much that Seneca should put these words into the mouth of Lucilius when reminiscing over the horrors of former days: " I risked my head for my loyalty. No word was wrung from me that I could not utter with a clear conscience. All my fears were for my friends, none for myself, except the fear of not proving a true friend." It speaks much for one who could retain the affection of such a coterie during eight years of official disgrace; and to this disposition can be attributed his (now lost) essay *On the Maintenance of Friendship.*

Germanicus, striving manfully to control mutineers in Germany and to forge his way to the mouth of the Elbe, could scarcely have foretold the criminal and distorted shapes into which his descendants would turn. His daughter, Agrippina, whose mother had for years followed her husband's war chariot and had borne him nine children, was unlucky enough to wed Domitius Ahenobarbus, the roughest and wildest beast of the Roman aristocracy. To this second " Ulysses in petticoats," mother of Nero, her uncle Claudius was attracted; after the removal of Messalina he sheepishly announced to the Senate his intention to marry her. Thus it was that Britannicus, son of Claudius and Messalina, soon dropped from sight, and Nero became heir presumptive, backed and fostered by his mother's forceful wiles. Nero was twelve years of age in 49,— ready for lessons in government. In this way Seneca, a former friend of the children of Germanicus, found himself the guardian of that hero's grandson in all matters of education and statecraft. The highest offices were entrusted to Seneca in rapid succession; money flowed into his purse through imperial donations and wise investments. He wrote speeches from and for the throne, in a style which appealed to Roman ears. Among his masterpieces may be counted the *De Clementia,* a companion piece to the *De Beneficiis,* and a model of wise counsel in moderate kingship which Nero might have followed more faithfully and with better results. Had Nero listened to his guidance he might have separated the private and the public rights of an emperor with more justice, and have restored some of the valuable attributes of the republican Senate by sundering its pre-

rogatives from those of the prince and giving
it a more legitimate use of authority.

By the year 60, therefore, Seneca was, in the
words of the Elder Pliny, " the leader in letters
and the leader in government." He interpreted
the laws and administered the state, wisely
leaving military matters to his trusted friend
Burrus, the prefect of the Praetorian Guard.
And for the years from 55 to 60 Rome was
governed as she had seldom been governed before,— passing the inspection of a rigid critic,
the Emperor Trajan, who declared that the
Quinquennium Neronis was the ideal epoch of
Roman history. And this was true; for during
that time Nero followed the counsel of these
two advisers.

Nero boasted that in the year 62 he had
saved the state sixty million sesterces ($3,000,-
000). But he might have given credit where
credit was due. Seneca had put the Treasury
heads on a three-year instead of a one-year
basis, thus saving experimentation in favor of
experience. Tacitus tells us that economy was
his watch-word. He reduced the percentage
given to the prosecutors of illegal wills; he
decreed in 58 a permanent court for the investigation of graft in provincial tax-raising, instead

of allowing personal lawsuits and the throat-
cutting of rival parties; he refused to condemn
unheard freedmen who were guilty of "in-
gratitude" toward their former masters. There
were no treason cases of the old sort during
his ministry, and he was probably instrumental
in sending the great general Corbulo to the
East. Moreover, in handling the energetic
Agrippina, he seems to have displayed the
greatest finesse. When the Armenian ambassa-
dors were about to present their credentials and
Agrippina had stepped forward to receive them,
a quick whisper from Seneca to Nero postponed her presumptuous action and put off the
audience. Seneca wrote Nero's first, and
probably many subsequent speeches from the
throne. When Nero wished to discharge the
honest and faithful Burrus for not consenting
to the murder of Nero's mother, Seneca came
to the rescue by prompting Burrus to declare
that he would execute her provided the treason
should be fully proved at a legal trial and that
any other conspirators should suffer the same
penalty. There was flattery, and there were
sharp corners to turn; but there was genius at
the wheel of the Roman state, keeping down the
tendency to crime and cruelty which forever

threatened in the breast of the young tiger-cub on the throne. Seneca knew well enough that a one-man government had its perils, and that a return to the republican system was impossible. The wonder is, not how he came to the end of the experiment in philosopher-kingship so soon, but how he managed to keep it in running order so long. For, as Aristotle remarks in several passages of his *Politics,* it is only in the ideal or perfect state that the virtues of the good citizen and the good man are identical.

But the task of this *ministre malgré lui* was very uphill work. Flattery was often resorted to: when a comet of unusual significance displayed itself, Seneca heralded it as of good omen, " redeeming comets from their bad character " because it appeared during the reign of Nero. The Emperor was cajoled into virtue, or rather out of vice, by means known to the skilful counsellor. And the grind of it all was admitted in the last book of Seneca, where he says: " Vice can be acquired even without a tutor." To what else than his attempts to keep Nero's crooked character straight are to be ascribed the ultimate disfavour and downfall of Nero's guardian?

The death of Burrus in 62 removed Seneca's chief aid to good government. At this period begins the process to which Pliny alludes when he tells us that Seneca's power had grown to such an extent that it came crashing down upon him. How far the two leaders had been consulted in Agrippina's murder can never be clearly known; but an honest look through history reveals them as at least not forbidding or protesting against the ultimate deed. Tigellinus had stepped upon the stage, aided and abetted by Poppaea, the notorious winner of Nero's heart and the prime cause of Agrippina's end. Seneca saw at this time that he could do no more, and begged for the privilege of retiring into private life, in order to travel, to compose his *Natural History*, and to complete the *Epistles*, but Nero kept him dangling in a state of doubt. Finally came the conspiracy of Piso, that indolent, popular, and democratic noble whom many of Nero's enemies wished to elevate to the purple,— a conspiracy in which all the Seneca brothers were supposed to be implicated,— and the last days of our philosopher, as sketched in the immortal description of Tacitus: [5]

" A centurion was sent to announce to

Seneca that his last hour was come. Seneca, undismayed, asked for his will; but this the centurion refused. Then turning to his friends he called them to witness that ' Being forbidden to requite them for their services, he was leaving to them the sole, and yet the noblest possession that remained to him: the pattern of his life. If they bore that in mind, they would win for themselves a name for virtue as the reward of their devoted friendship.' At one moment he would check their tears with conversation; at another he would brace up their courage by high-strung language of rebuke, asking — ' Where was now their philosophy? ' . . . ' To whom was Nero's cruelty unknown? What was left for one who had murdered his mother and his brother but to slay his guardian and teacher also? ' . . . His wife announced her resolve to die with him. Seneca would not thwart her noble ambition; and he loved her too dearly to expose her to insult after he was gone. . . . ' Let us both share the fortitude in thus nobly dying; but thine shall be the noblest end.' . . . A single incision with the knife opened the arm of each. . . . Worn out at last by the pain, and fearing to break down his wife's courage by his suffering,

[27]

or to lose his own self-command at the sight of hers, he begged her to move into another chamber. But even in his last moments his eloquence did not fail. He called his secretaries to his side and dictated to them many things which being published in his own words I deem it needless to reproduce. . . . Meanwhile Seneca, in the agonies of a slow and lingering death, implored Statius Annaeus, his tried and trusted friend and physician, to produce a poison with which he had long provided himself, being the same as that used for public executions at Athens. The draught was brought, but the limbs were too cold, the body too numb, to let the poison act. At last, he was put into a warm bath, and as he sprinkled the slaves about him he added: ' This libation is to Jupiter the Liberator! ' He was then carried into the hot vapor bath, and perished by suffocation. His body was burnt without any funeral ceremony, in accordance with instructions about his end which he had inserted in his will in the heyday of his wealth and power. "

Thus did Seneca win release. It had been with conviction that he wrote, shortly before, to a friend who was more independently situated:

[28]

" You have escaped the vices of the soul, the hypocrite's brow, the flatterer's speech fashioned to serve another's will, the dissembler's heart, the miser's spirit, which robs all but yet mortifies itself."

In April of the year 65 ended the career of one who made a brave attempt to join a theory of life with a practice of life. How successful the attempt was we shall never completely know; the pictures of the period are boldly drawn and usually with prejudice. We are presented on the one side with heroes like Thrasea and the school of Cato; upon the other is all the scandal which is popularly associated with Claudius and Nero. Our evidence from the early Empire is deficient and defective because men no longer talked facts as they did in Cicero's day; they upheld causes, or defended policies, or made language the veil for emotions which used to be expressed more obviously. Tacitus, Dio, Suetonius,[6]— keen painters all, but none of them contemporaries of the Nero epoch,— have left us a vivid picture. But we are compelled to draw our own conclusions. It is reasonable to believe that in this Spanish regent of the Roman world we have an historic figure,— compounded of business ability, keen statecraft, brilliant style and moving mind. Later Roman emperors respected him because of his reforms in administration; a Bossuet could quarry from his works in order to impress France with a steadier court-philosophy; Petrarch could look upon his letters as a basis for humanistic prose; and Emerson, as we have seen, could class him as one of the world's most inspiring masters of thought.

II. SENECA: HIS INFLUENCE
UPON PAGAN ROME

MR. FERRERO has frequently pointed
out the resemblance between the
early Roman Empire and the
United States of to-day. He has shown how
their finance, commerce, public works, public
opinion, and, along certain lines, government,
bear a similar relation to one another, and to
the community at large. Society was cosmopolitan and yet uniform; opinion was more or
less traditional. We shall see that Seneca ran
contrary to, or ahead of, current ideas in his
philosophy, in his style, and in his view of the
state,— that he was a popular figure in these
activities and yet provoked opposition among
those who accepted the old order as worth continuing. Hence at first he was a sort of east
wind among the sluggish thinkers of his time.
But he knew his Rome better than most native-
born Romans knew her. He took the encyclopaedic, the eclectic view. He felt the pulse
of coming ages better than court rhetoricians

[31]

(though he was one himself), better than historians, better than the conservatives of his day.

Opinions regarding the genius of Seneca vary from the outset. One of his enemies, whom he had punished for violating the rule that a lawyer should not plead cases for a cash consideration, called him " A dilettante, one who satisfies the crude minds of our youth, and who envies those who keep the good old eloquence alive for the purpose of defending Roman citizens! " The mad emperor Caligula accused him of producing " mere sophomoric exercises " and of developing a style that was " sand without lime." But in the very passage where Suetonius quotes these sallies, he speaks of Seneca as " all the rage in those days," and Columella, the writer on farming, calls him the leading vine-grower of Italy and a man of brilliant intellect. Seneca is known to the satirist Juvenal, who speaks of him three times with approval, and to Ausonius, three hundred years after, as " the multi-millionaire." To the emperor Trajan he is an administrator of great ability. But it took two hundred years for him to stand forth as a " friend and aider of those who would live in the spirit."

Then, as now, the literary world and the business world were far apart. Literature was in the hands of specialists, and the general public, especially in the age of Tiberius, was mentally starved. " After the time of Augustus," says Fronto, the associate and courtier of Marcus Aurelius one hundred years later, " ideas were threadbare and mouldy. And the emperors from Tiberius to Vespasian were as much ashamed of the spoken and written word as they were disgusted with morals and sorry for crimes." Something novel was necessary, and it was found in the development of the *elocutio novella,*— the Euphuism of Rome,— which began at this time to grow, and which burgeoned to its full bloom in the period of the Antonines. Seneca adapted the language of the business world to the artificial style of the scholar and man of letters.

It was exactly this habit to which three of his critics objected. One was a college professor, one an antiquary, and one a courtier,— all of them professionals, so to speak. Seneca was an amateur.

Quintilian the professor, who about the year 72 A.D. had been formally established by the emperor Vespasian head of rhetorical schools of Rome, shook his head sadly over Seneca's style. He seems to have felt the same concern regarding the danger of this influence upon the pens and minds of Roman youths that was felt seventy years ago by the cautious antagonists of Carlyle in England and America. He feared the New Style, and he clung to Cicero, just as the elder Seneca had clung some years before. But for both men it was a losing game; the innovator was to have his way for better or for worse. Theoretical oratory, with its "point" and epigram and mechanical skill, had come to stay. According to Quintilian's norm, therefore, we note his protest: "Seneca had many good qualities, . . . an easy flowing wit, plenty of industry, and a large stock of information. . . . In his philosophy he was not exhaustive, but he was a strong champion against vice. He has many noble sayings, and much that deserves reading for the sake of character-development. But, as I said, there are many ruinous elements in his style, because of his inclination to indulge in tricks. . . . By not being too fond of his own idea, by refraining from impairing the solidity of his subject-matter with over-refined subtleties, he might have won approval in the opinion of the learned as well as through his popularity with the younger element. The well-trained may read him, if only for the purpose of applying the critical faculty. . . . Our student should, however, pick and choose when reading Seneca, as I wish Seneca himself had done. For a nature that could get what it wished was worthy of wishing for better things."

Evidently a new and perhaps a dangerous star had swum into the Roman ken,— a subject of much discussion. We think not only of Carlyle above-mentioned, but of Macaulay, who stamped the review and the essay with a new combination of tricks and turns, force and dignity. Quintilian is fair to Seneca the man, but to the writer he shows himself a ribboned academician, ignoring the popular currents and striving for standards of old time. He forgot that in an age when the only piece of work rewarded by a certain emperor was a banquet-dialogue between a mushroom, a reed-bird, and an oyster, an author who hoped to gain a hearing must devise something striking. And such was the case in the reign of Tiberius, when Seneca began to write. Struggle as the Conservatives might, the Ciceronian norm was no more to be revived in Roman literary history. Thus from the unoriginal sameness of the Tiberian age emerged Seneca the innovator, the early advocate of a Silver Latin style.

Winning a prominent position as lawyer and orator during the reign of Caligula, he had cast about for a medium in which his message to society might be most effective. After experimenting with such topics as *De Superstitione, De Matrimonio,* and similar subjects in which learning was popularized to suit the cultivated people of Rome, he had found his medium in a modification of the Diatribe. In his hands this became the popular Essay, and is the first real and consistent example of that which in English literature we denominate Essay. The Diatribe, later to become fashionable in the hands of show-speakers like Dio of the Golden Mouth, satisfied what we might call the " University Extension " element in the Roman world. It was partly historical discourse, partly literary display, and partly oratory of the fictitious court-room type which was so popular after free speech had been muzzled. The study of this question-answer type of literature, broadly speaking, was the college training of every young Roman; and a glance at the Memoirs of Seneca's father will show us what an array of stylistic artificiality was spread before the future citizen. St. Paul himself, with his convincing presentation of doctrine and dogma, aptly illustrated and armed with answers to all possible questions, may be described as a master of Diatribe. It is this very type that Seneca loosened into Essay. The medium which did not demand the close thought or the detailed knowledge required by philosophy or technical treatises, and yet kept the reader on the *qui vive,* exactly suited the nervous, bored, and clever Roman world. We have just seen what Quintilian thought of the effect of these popular essays upon contemporary youth. As the college student spent his time in debating legal casuistries, so Seneca took over the debate-motif into philosophy, seasoning it with current problems and bits of Stoicism. *Why do good men suffer evil if there is a just Providence? What is the Happy Life? The True Leisure. Anger and how to Control it. On Cures for Ill Fortune. On the Shortness of Life.* These and kindred discussions are Essays, a new type to the Roman, who used to do his thinking along such lines in poetry, or treatises, or autobiography, or fragmentarily in letters to his friends. In this field Seneca is therefore a pioneer who " combined all moods, inventing one."

The *Epistles* of Seneca are the high-water mark of this subjective essay. They lead the way for Medieval Latin declarations of literary independence, catching some of the Oriental individualism which marks the man with a message. They discard the Greek communal element and make toward self-revelation, just as Montaigne many years later discarded previous types and spoke as a definite personality. They develop themselves round a central and subjective mood,— contrary to the diary-fashion of Cicero's correspondence which is always concrete and, in spite of Cicero's egotism, full of objective comment, like Evelyn and Walpole. And precisely the reason why certain of his later critics objected to him is because he sacrificed everything to the point of the idea under discussion, becoming, unlike his Roman predecessors, abstract rather than concrete.

One example will suffice. Cicero skips from general matters to objective affairs: " In your letter you ask whether I take more pleasure in hills and a view or a walk by the silver sea. . . . Upon my word, both are so beautiful that I doubt which to prefer." And then comes a discussion of Brutus, salted down with Homeric quotations. All is " rambly " and delightful,— the *disjecta membra* of a statesman's mind. Seneca's attack is so very different: " I am resting at the country house which once belonged to Scipio Africanus himself; and I write to you after doing reverence to his spirit, at an altar which I am inclined to think is his tomb. . . . What can I do but admire his magnanimity? . . . I have inspected the house . . . the well . . . the bath. . . . But who in these days could bear to bathe in such humble fashion? We think ourselves poor and mean if our walls are not resplendent. . . . How some persons nowadays condemn Scipio as a boor because he did not let daylight into the bath through wide windows. . . . ' Poor fool,' they say, ' he did not know how to live! '. . . I learned a valuable lesson from the present owner of this villa, that a tree can be transplanted, no matter how far gone in years." The whole essay of Seneca (Bacon called all the *Epistles* " Essaies ") proceeds from concrete to abstract and plays about one single point, the vigor, simplicity, and agricultural interests of a typical early Roman,

[39]

just as Charles Lamb is uniform when he describes " Mackery End in Hertfordshire " or as Stevenson is uniform when he rambles by a French river or muses in a portrait-gallery over ruddy-faced Scotch admirals.

In short, Seneca was a puzzle to most of his contemporaries. He wrote a prose essay which could not be identified with any contemporary type of literature; it was not normal Stoicism, like the work of Epictetus; it was not the Lamb-like style soon to be exemplified in the Younger Pliny; it was not rhetoric *par excellence,* as in the treatises of his father; nor was it the trenchant description of Cicero. And yet it can be proved, by a sort of paradox, that this very mixing of types, this habit of scorning the " liturgical " form, has resulted in the catholicity of his appeal to so many thinkers in subsequent ages.

That Seneca had an eye to his contemporaries rather than to his predecessors is proved by the remarks of Aulus Gellius, an antiquarian of the second century. Gellius was a sort of Isaac D'Israeli, who gathered into his random essays (*Nights in Athens*) a scramble of interesting gossip and history which throws much light on the customs of the period.

People had begun again to *archaize,* to hark back to ancient Rome for their models; and Gellius takes umbrage at the patronizing remarks of Seneca on Cicero, Ennius, and Virgil: " I need not judge him in general, but we really need to consider what he says about these three authors . . . he picks out some verses by Ennius and says of them: ' I am surprised that men of the greatest eloquence, enthusiasts for Ennius, have praised this trash as if it were of the best quality.' . . . The nonsensical trifler says: ' These were not Cicero's faults; they were the faults of his age.' . . . And furthermore: ' Even our poet Virgil put in some grating verses so that the people might recognize an antiquated element in a new poem.' . . . Young men may be as enthusiastic as they will. . . . But you can still find a clever thing or two in his works."

Again, therefore, testimony appears with regard to his *ingenium,* or *ingyne,* as Ben Jonson and the Elizabethans used to call it. Gellius was a lover of antiquity, looking backward; Seneca was teeming with the future, looking forward.

The third critic, however, was still more redolent of antiquity. Fronto, as any one will discover on reading Pater's *Marius the Epicurean,* was a literary man, a courtier, and a stylist, a citizen of the place and age when over-refinement had become supreme in Roman letters; but an archaizer borrowing from the Republican Sallust and the earlier gallery of worthies like Cato, whose clauses he supposed to be sounder, although many of his own distortions reveal the evil results of artificial coalitions in phraseology. Fronto accuses Seneca of " jog-trot sentences," " glaring patches," " sugar plums," " easy lapses into slippery ways." This intimate of Marcus Aurelius sought the artistic bouquet of old Republican style; the result is that all is artificiality in him, while Seneca, confessedly " the author whom one finds most frequently in the hands of young men," keeps pace with the times, and even outruns his age.

The summary of all this criticism seems to be a due deference to the wit and wisdom and force of the author under fire, but deprecation of his radicalism in thought and in style. The critics did not understand one who combined Plato and Stoicism, who filled letters with scientific treatise-matter, who founded the Essay, who put popular idioms into dignified literature, and who stepped from the office to the study as readily as Mr. Balfour steps from Downing Street into studies in Theism and Humanism.

There is but a short path now to the end of creative Roman literature. Plutarch, the peer of Seneca in Montaigne's opinion, seems to have known little about him (which is an absurd supposition), or else to have lacked interest in one whose concern was with the present, who stood for a new order of things, and who did not belong to the gallery of worthies from Greece and Rome. Boethius dislikes " the Epicurean herd, the Stoics, and the rest." Macrobius, who lived at the turn of the fourth century and was a sort of warmed-over Gellius, was far enough away in years to pilfer several passages from Seneca without acknowledgment, and thus tacitly to take him for granted. Every one admits his prominence in general, but most of these successors fail to classify him as a standard literary authority.

Tacitus gives us a post-mortem examination into the political controversies wherein Seneca played so large a part. He sketches him strikingly, but not unfavorably. Seneca is adroit,

clever in style as in politics; and he is complimented indirectly by being attacked through
the agency of the *deteriores,* the opposition
party, and especially of one Suillius, who
mounts the stump on all occasions, a man whose
character, like his name, is not above suspicion.
Suillius evidently represented the reactionaries,
who feared the new system of government
which Seneca and Burrus were maintaining.
There were several reasons why this opposition
took place.

Seneca, like Cicero, Napoleon, and Lincoln,
was a *novus homo.* This name had for centuries
been applied by the Romans to those whose
family had never before been included in of-
ficialdom and the governing caste, to those
whose halls contained no busts of departed
senators. Furthermore, he came at a time
when the machine of Augustus was a thing of
the past, when a weaker Senate or an eccentric
Emperor or a threatening army rendered
necessary a careful balancing of statecraft and
tradition, and when rich freedmen of foreign
antecedents had control of all the expert details
of bureaucracy. There was no man-for-man
responsibility in the Empire, as there was in
the Republic which had conquered Hannibal

or brought the Mediterranean under the sway of Rome. Patricians and plebeians no longer heckled one another from the opposition benches; there was a self-satisfied aristocracy, and a proletariat whose sole aim was to be fed and amused. Hence, from the year 50 A.D. the problem was how to make the court function in relation to the state, how to balance imperial caprice with efficiency of administration, how to interpret Rome at a time when elections were a farce and the professional politician was the only instrument.

The new feature of Seneca's activity was the fact that he represented the cabinet system of government in which he performed or superintended most of the functions of such a system in his own person. Unlike Augustus, Maecenas, and Agrippa, who divided up the duties of Empire, Seneca, except for the Praetorian Guard and the policing of the city, seems to have gained by degrees the whole control of Rome.

Upon the prime minister, therefore, rested the responsibility of guiding a prince whose power was in practice unlimited. And the difficulty lay in the fact that Seneca's own power was not specific but depended upon the original invitation of Claudius and Agrippina, upon the coöperation of several rich and able freedmen whom he had to keep balanced one against the other, and upon the momentum of the provincial administration. At the death of Claudius in 54 he was supreme, and master of the situation as long as he could harmonize the discordant elements in the state. It seems that he succeeded in doing this for seven or eight years,— a magnificent experiment. Nero was malleable and popular in his youth. Seneca's method of handling him was frequent counsel, given in writing and with entire publicity. Tacitus mentions many speeches composed for Nero on occasions of state, but most interesting of all is the *De Clementia,* which was brought out shortly after the prince's accession to the throne, and which is compounded of skilful advice, flattery, and reminders of the responsibility under which an emperor must always rest. " You must consider attentively this enormous throng, quarrelsome, mutinous, and wayward. You must reflect that *if it breaks the yoke* it will sweep along to its own undoing as well as to the ruin of others." . . . One of the chief contributions of the Prime Minister to the science of good government is his oft-repeated doctrine, expressed both in this work and elsewhere, that the revolutionary violence of earlier days, built upon individual force, is responsible for all the evils of history, and that intelligent coöperation in the control of a self-denying ruler is the solution of the problem. " Julius Caesar involved himself so closely with the commonwealth that neither could be extricated without ruining both; for the ruler needs backing, and the state needs control." *Mansuetudo*, or human sympathy, is the keynote of the treatise; this quality must be seasoned with intelligence of the highest order. The clemency of Nero must be original, and not like the " tired-out cruelty " of Augustus, who adopted a pacific policy after wading through the blood of several revolutions. Seneca knew his Romans: " No animal is more pettish, or more in need of skilful handling, or more to be humoured, than man." It was a far cry, as we have said before, back to the citizen-farmer of the early Republic; the whole cosmopolitan world-mob sat in the amphitheatre or received its dole of grain on stated days.

The work is not startlingly original in its separate ideas; in fact it is full of tiresome repetitions; but it is replete with a new spirit. Burrus, the commander of the Praetorian Guard, is complimented, not as the head of an army but as the wise controller of a police system. And the whole message of the imperial tutor is a plea for understanding, for a new slate, for a point of view which will give every Roman some opportunity to make choices, to take more part in government, and to gain greater freedom in life, liberty, and the pursuit of happiness. We shall call attention, later, to the influence of this pamphlet upon Calvin and its significance in the theocratic history of the sixteenth century. The " good emperors," from Nerva through Marcus Aurelius, are under an obligation to Seneca for this experiment in government; and it was but a natural relapse toward the revolutionary period when Rome was compelled to endure the vagaries of the later Nero, the bloody year of 68–9, and the cruelties of Domitian. It was of course more logical for power to be constitutionally centered in the hands of a strong Emperor like Trajan, than for a weak monarch to be propped by an adviser, no matter how intelligent or conscientious the latter might be. But this very centralization provoked the ire of those who thought that the good old days of senatorial participation might return.

Pliny the Elder comes to our minds the instant we think of ancient science. And yet Pliny himself acknowledges Seneca [7] to be an authority on marine zoölogy, geology, earthquakes, and meteorology. We have seen that the latter was also a geographer, having begun his investigations early, recorded his observations in Egypt, and made a study of the peoples of India. Pliny is the more highly regarded now; but throughout the Middle Ages the *Naturales Quaestiones,* or *Natural History,* of Seneca was the chief textbook, outranking all the Bestiaries and Physiologi which formed educational pabulum for monastery-schools and for the children of the better classes. The difference between the two writers is that Seneca speculates more on his own account, while Pliny's work includes art, botany, mineralogy, and everything that we now classify under the head of biology, tabulated with the greatest care and with acknowledgment to every author laid under contribution. Studies of volcanoes and earthquakes, with their common origin, the source of the Nile, reasons for thunder, winds, waters, and comets are the work of Seneca the observer, sometimes blundering, sometimes making a lucky hit, but always inquisitive and seeming to understand rather than merely to catalogue what others have said. Even in his other works Seneca shows the same inquiring mind: in the 57th *Epistle,* which describes a journey through the famous Naples tunnel, the " Crypta Neapolitana," he speculates upon the air currents and the mental effect of contrasts in light and darkness. The mind of Seneca was curious and original; his physics contributed to his own philosophy. With all his Stoicism he was a pluralist at heart, like William James; he could tolerate no generalities which were irrevocable, but made up his world from his own personal investigations and ideas. He was indebted to Aristotle's *Meteorology,* to Theophrastus, to Aratus, to Varro; he may have compared notes and collaborated with Pliny, whose work was published twelve years after Seneca's death. He is refreshingly undogmatic, incomplete, and at times even senile. We cannot rightly accuse him of all the moralizing and dogmatism which spoiled the objective accuracy of medieval Science before Roger Bacon. Nor can we blame him for assuming that imprisoned air is the main agency in earthquakes, or for not knowing that the rainbow's colors are the result of decomposition of white light instead of a seeming color which does not really exist, or for believing that lightning melts metals and freezes wine, or that the sun is supported by exhalations from the earth. In his assumption, however, that comets may have orbits which carry them beyond the zodiac, that there is an evolutionary process in the world, and that rings round the sun are often the result of atmospheric conditions, he is sound. But after all, how accurate were the astronomers before Galileo, the physicists before Newton, or the biologists before Darwin? Seneca's guesses are as good as those of any other speculator before the discoveries of modern Science.

He wrote for later ages rather than for Rome. He was the *primus artifex* of a point of view which conventional Rome did not understand. Perhaps this was because his writing was so occasional; he had tossed off tragedies to relieve the dreariness of exile; he had put together essays for purposes of consolation or personal relief; he had made himself a master of science; and in the *Epistles,* his greatest work, he had sought to sink himself in philosophy and quietism, and thus be rid of a haunting burden,— association with Nero in the government of the Roman Empire. To himself and his contemporaries he was a clever stylist and man of affairs; to us he is a philosopher.

III. HOW HE APPEALED TO
THE CHURCH

I T IS the Christian writers, the early Fathers
of the growing Christian Church, who elevate Seneca into prominence as more than
a man of affairs or an author of questionable
style. When the new religion has ceased to
be a secret ritual and has risen superior to the
worship of Jupiter Capitolinus, we find that the
subject of this sketch is as warmly welcomed
as he was formerly abused. But it is for a
different reason. The leaders of the Church
were less interested in a way of saying things
than in the thing to be said; they were desirous
of winning over as many educated converts as
possible to the new faith. In Seneca they discovered a thinker who struck to the root of
their problem, whose language and traditions
appealed to them as citizeins both of Rome and
of the City not built with hands. East and
West could meet through the message of such
an interpreter, especially along religious
lines. The lapse of time had wiped out

cliques in literature and politics; the lasting qualities of the man were all that mattered; and at this point the criterion became one of religion and religion only, for several centuries. St. Jerome himself had said: " If you read all the books of the philosophers you cannot help finding in them some part of the vessels of God." [8] But Seneca was placed above Cicero in this category.

The reasons for this are not far to seek. Seneca was a Stoic, and Stoicism was the porch to Christianity. Then, as now, it was the thought-force that lay nearest to our inspirational religion. It was Stoicism which made the Christian fathers claim Seneca as one of their own, which made St. Paul quote Aratus to the Athenians as one " in whom we live and move and have our being." There is Stoicism in the *Invictus* of W. E. Henley and in the *No Coward Soul is Mine* of Emily Brontë. Wordsworth is full of it:

> " A *sense sublime*
> *Of something far more deeply interfused,*
> *A motion and a spirit that impels*
> *All thinking things, all objects of all thought,*
> *And rolls through all things."*

William James, greatest of American philosophers, is in harmony therewith: "I feel that we are Nature's through and through, that we are wholly conditioned; that not a wiggle of our will happens save as the result of physical laws; and yet, notwithstanding, we are *en rapport* with reason. . . . It is not that we are all nature *but* some point which is reason, but that all is nature *and* all is reason too." And John Morley says to us: "An open-hearted Stoicism is no bankrupt or useless thing." Stoicism, more than the plant-and-animal studies of the Peripatetics, more than the vague realism of the Academics, more than the *laissez-faire* of the Epicureans, had struck home to the Roman mind. It had taken the fancy of the Scipionic circle because it combined idealism with citizenship. It took by storm the Romans of the Empire who wished by free will to think themselves into another world, and sometimes to betake themselves thither voluntarily. It had run the blockade of the Alexandrian age and had escaped unscathed as a workable philosophy, compounded of most of the other creeds. Cousin tells us that all philosophies change in a regular cycle of Sensationalism, Idealism, Scepticism, and Mysticism. The essence of the Stoic philosophy is its combination of these four phases, and this explains its consequent lasting power.

The Stoics, who for three hundred years before Seneca's time had been building up a creed, now adding to their doctrines and now subtracting, believed that knowledge was attainable. They began where the Epicureans stopped, with the sensations. These, they held, produced a " mind picture," which led to the concept, and from the concept came knowledge. One of their earlier masters compared this process first to the open palm, then to the curved fingers, then to the closed fist, and finally to the fist clasped tightly in the other hand — resulting in knowledge, the gift only of the wise man. Whether the process of thus assimilating and developing sensation into science was correct, could be tested only by reason, logic, and will-power. The machinery of speech, the sequence of right thinking, and unity with the spirit of the universe were the three ways which answered the Sceptics and Epicureans and offered a solution in the face of the learned doubt of the Academics. In the last analysis the " inward touch " must be present: this corresponded with the inspirational " daemon " of Socrates, the inner light of Thomas à Kempis and the Quakers, and the visions of St. Paul.

Stoicism acknowledged Deity and welcomed it. Stoicism bade its followers take part in the duties of family and citizenship. It prescribed no monastic or eccentric rules, and upheld all the features of life that men regard as desirable. Virtue alone was good; but office, wealth, influence, and worldly enjoyments were " advantageous," provided they did not break down the moral fiber of the possessor. Only, they must in the last resort be recognized as non-essentials. Evil was an incidental; good conduct was the only criterion. The soul, part of the World-Spirit, was immortal in the sense of non-perishability: how far it was individually immortal was often debated, and by none more than by Seneca.

Such are the general ideas associated with Stoicism. Different exponents argued differently on its various phases: one placed the whole function in perfect reasoning and syllogistic accuracy; another interpreted life by Nature as the sole guide; another abandoned the perfection-theory and admitted worldly considerations as on a par with virtue; and at the end of the Roman Republic we find scientific study and eclectic combinations overcoming the absolutism of the Greek founders. But Stoicism was a spiritual, progressive, and optimistic creed. The hymn of Cleanthes [9] gives us this spirit:

" *Glory would some through bitter strife attain,*
And some are eager after lawless gain;
Some lust for sensual delights, but each
Finds that too soon his pleasure turns to pain.

But, Zeus all-bountiful! The thunder-flame
And the dark cloud thy majesty proclaim:
From ignorance deliver us, that leads
The sons of men to sorrow and to shame.

Wherefore dispel it, Father, from the soul
And grant that Wisdom may our life control,
Wisdom which teaches Thee to guide the world
Upon the path of justice to its goal.

So winning honor Thee shall we requite
With love, lauding still thy works of might;
Since gods nor men find worthier meed than
this —
The universal Law to praise aright."

When Seneca, after flirting in his youth with Pythagoreanism (especially because of its vegetarian doctrine) and with certain of the eastern cults, took up Stoicism, the creed which he adopted had been a favorite one at Rome for nearly two hundred years. We have seen its influence on the Scipionic circle; we know that gradually its world-citizenship developed the " law of nations " as contrasted with the state law of Rome, and that much of Mediterranean cosmopolitanism is due to the Stoic *ius gentium*. What influence it had upon the actual government of Rome may be gauged from Cato the Younger, from Seneca himself, from Marcus Aurelius, and from the reactions which it produced in the case of the Emperor Domitian, who refused its advances and ejected its upholders from Rome — Epictetus among others. And Cicero himself, who always looked upon Stoicism with favor, helped to make it fashionable in cultivated circles. It is sufficient to mention Brutus, the tyrannicide, in order to show how strongly its leaven was working on the theory of statecraft. Finally, the very parodies of Horace, like the quips of Addison upon London fashions, show to what an extent Stoicism had taken hold upon the " progressive " second-raters of the day: " growing the beard of wisdom " ; " none but

the wise man is sane " ; " the wise man is
second only to Jupiter, rich, free, respected,
handsome, king of kings, and more sound
than anyone else,— except when he has hay-
fever! "

Seneca is unique in his interpretation [10] of
this Stoic philosophy because to so marked
a degree he admits into it the theories of
other schools. " One may debate with Socrates, be skeptical with Carneades, overcome human frailty with the Stoics, or go
beyond it with the Cynics; — since the universe allows us to go into partnership with
all the ages." " I cross over into the
enemy's camp (Epicurus), not as a deserter,
but as a scout." The first thirty-three
Epistles, and many parts of his dialogues are
linked with the name of Epicurus: " In my
own opinion Epicurus is really a strong man,
even though he did wear long sleeves."
" These utterances do not belong to Epicurus;
they are common property." " I will say, in
the teeth of the Stoic school, that the counsels
of Epicurus are holy and righteous, and if you
inspect them closely, puritanic: he thins down
pleasure and assigns to it the same rules that
we assign to virtue — namely, obedience to

Nature." " I shall use the old road; but if I find one that makes a shorter cut and is smoother to travel, I shall open the new road." This attitude may be contrasted with Cicero's regular scorn of a school which seemed to him self-indulgent and mentally indolent.

Again, Seneca has a profound respect for Plato. The 58th *Epistle* is devoted to Plato's doctrine of existence and to his Theory of Ideas; the 65th bows to Aristotle and Plato, while defending the Stoic plan of Matter and God. The later Academic school is criticized as " having introduced a new knowledge — non-knowledge " ; but the idealism of Plato — the thought that if the transcendental soul is not recognized, all thought and contemplation are futile — runs through Seneca's prose writings as a consistent thread.

Pythagoreanism was essentially eccentric in the early empire. And yet Seneca began by following two leads of this school and by observing the usual vegetarian apprenticeship. " The days of my youth coincided with the rule of Tiberius; and at that time foreign rituals were being expelled from the city. Among proofs of their superstitious influence was abstinence from animal food. So at the request

of my father, who feared a bad name rather
than disliked philosophy, I returned to my
former habits. It was not hard for him to persuade me to dine more luxuriously! " Hence,
ever retaining a respect for " the silent and
holy retreat of Pythagoras," Seneca turned to
Stoicism and studied under its two leading
contemporary interpreters.

One who reads Seneca's prose writings, however, with a detachment from the ultra-theo-
retical points of view will note that perhaps
the strongest bond with any past master of philosophy is that with Posidonius. This scientist,
whose writings have come down to us only
in scattered fragments, was mainly responsible
for the spreading of Stoicism throughout the
Roman world in the first century B.C., for the
scientific spirit which made so strong an
appeal to Seneca, and for the flexible tone of
the school as contrasted with the logic-haunted
works of the early Greek founders. For example, while returning to the old theory that
the universe is destroyed by fire and recreated
at periodic intervals, and while accepting
divination and the rituals of sacrifice, he
" Baconizes " philosophy by making scientific
observation the most important element and

by admitting the specific rules of conduct which so many philosophers regarded as outside the pale of the Stoic creed proper. The whole 90th *Epistle* is occupied with debating Posidonius' contention that the inventions and discoveries of early man were the result of philosophy, and with maintaining that philosophy is not so closely connected with arts and crafts. Perhaps the question may be begged. Perhaps we may say that it all depends on the definition, just as the "natural philosophy" of fifty years ago has now to be explained as "physics." Seneca pays Posidonius the compliment of analyzing his contention carefully, although he disagrees with him. But in the same letter he speaks of him as "of the number of those who have contributed the most to philosophy."

Seneca therefore tones down the extremes of Stoicism; he does for the first century of the Empire what Posidonius had done for the last century of the Republic. He found Roman religion mere mummery; he therefore abandoned divination and sacrifice in favor of communion and prayer: "We do not need to uplift our hands towards heaven, or to beg the keeper of a temple to let us approach the idol's ear, as if in this way our prayers were more likely to be heard." "Nothing is shut off from the sight of God. He is witness of our souls and He comes into the very midst of our thoughts." He smiles away many of the paradoxes which we have seen that Horace burlesqued; he devotes whole chapters to proving that cast-iron syllogisms are of no avail for one who seeks the higher truth,— just as Benedetto Croce in recent years bade us forget the lifeless abstractions which marred the philosophy of fifty years ago: "I adhere to my testimony, that this sort of proof does not please me. It is shameful for one to go forth to battle on behalf of gods and men, armed only with an awl!" He admits that "soul" may, according to the older Stoic view, be defined as "substance" or "body"; and when he finishes the argument, destroys its logic by establishing the spirituality of "soul." And, amid the debate as to the soul's imperishability,— whether it is crushed out of us at death, whether it survives as a fiery particle, whether there is a sort of part-time immortality, or whether it remains as a personality after being freed from the prison-body,— he

concludes for a future life, with all the glory
of reward for life nobly lived.

The allusions, in Seneca's *Epistles* alone, to
a single deity, would be sufficient to strike
a Church Father with a kinship of common
interests and beliefs. Many a Pagan philosopher had made God more unified and personal.
Epictetus had said: " God is within, and your
daemon is within," often bearing witness to
concentrated divinity rather than to the poly-
theism of his predecessors. Plato himself
tended in that direction: Socrates and his Holy
Guide are very near to the Christian soul. But
Seneca said the same thing in a manner which
these Romans could understand and apply:
" God is near you, he is with you. . . . A
holy spirit indwells within us, one who marks
our good and bad deeds, and is our guardian."
Or, " Why should you not believe that something of divinity exists in one who is a part of
God? All this universe which encompasses us
is one, and it is God; we are associates of God;
we are his members: " — fundamental Stoic
doctrine no doubt, but clothed in Christian
language. Examine the works of St. Ambrose,
and you will see how many Stoic elements

form the background of his arguments. Consider the connection of St. Augustine's *servitus dei est summa libertas* with Seneca's Epicurean borrowing: *philosophiae servias oportet, ut tibi contingat vera libertas*. Note also how other writers take over the four virtues into Christianity, and build a new edifice upon the old foundation: "The four rivers of Eden represent the four virtues,— prudence, temperance, courage, and justice." When, therefore, M. Lévy-Bruhl [11] analyzes Seneca's ideas of Deity, showing that *Deus ipse se fecit* is an advance on the "nature," "fate," and "fortune" definitions of his Stoic predecessors, that this God contains more of reason than of fatalism, that Lactantius recognizes the congeniality of St. Peter's God with Seneca's, and that the God as thus portrayed is a more human God than any other Stoic divinity, we see at once the reason why Tertullian called Seneca "ours." In fact it is through Lactantius that we know of Seneca's *Exhortationes* and his *De Immatura Morte*. And so it goes. There is, in reality, nothing ancient and nothing modern where the Eternal is concerned.

Many of these early Christians, scholars

trained in the classic school, felt the charm of the old pagan writings, as St. Augustine, for example, was ravished by the beauty of Cicero's *Hortensius* and by the romance of Dido's tragic end. Minucius Felix, the first Roman who holds a literary brief for Christianity, consciously and unconsciously echoes Seneca; and Lactantius patterns one of his themes upon the opening of the *De Providentia,* wherein the world-old question is discussed: why the wise man who is captain of his own soul is compelled to suffer affliction while the baser sort go scot-free. This question had been asked by Job and the Psalmist, and repeated itself down through Fénelon and the great French preachers. It was Seneca's modern and forward-looking note that appealed to the early Church; and that is perhaps why they passed over the heads of pagan saints like Epictetus and selected our philosopher as their advocate in the foreign ranks.

This idea of similarity was pushed to an extreme in two cases, the one, a myth of Messianic tendencies which was seriously discussed by a German scholar forty years ago, and the other a fabrication of a correspondence between Seneca and the Apostle Paul. The forgery (a pious one, to be sure) dates perhaps from the fourth century, although it was not long ago that the series of letters was regarded as genuine. No doubt St. Paul was in Rome during Seneca's life-time, and it is not inconceivable that they may have met and exchanged ideas. We know that in his youth Seneca expressed an interest in non-Roman cults; it is impossible that the prime minister of the Empire should have been in entire ignorance of a worship that caught the attention of all Rome by its unusual features and its ascetic practices. It may have been one of the estranging elements between Nero and his minister; and it is possible that the martyrdoms may have led to Seneca's resignation. Conversely, as we have no positive evidence one way or another, we might, if we were confronted with facts that now lie buried, be compelled to blush for Seneca as an accomplice in the whole cruel business. But we cannot follow certain biographers who uphold the latter point of view. These fourteen letters, eight by the Roman and six by Paul, contain such anachronisms as an appreciation of the latter's epistle to the Galatians, a chatty account of the great fire of the year 64, and a style that would have set on edge the teeth of both men, who were instinctive writers of force and cultivation, geniuses both. But such a test was not necessary in the eyes of later Christians; they had discovered one who spoke and wrote from the same ethical standard as their own.

Another connection is Seneca's brother Gallio, the Gallio of Acts 18, 11–17, who on a famous occasion decided that " these matters were out of his province." The gentle and popular Gallio, Governor of the Greek province of Achaia from 51 to 52 A.D., presided at the court before which St. Paul appeared as a defendant, accused of illegal religious practices.

" *One thing only I see most clear,*
  As I pray you also see.
  Claudius Caesar hath set me here
  Rome's deputy to be.
  It is her peace that ye go to break —
  Not mine, nor any king's,
  But, touching your clamour of ' Conscience sake,'
  I care for none of these things."

" *Whether ye rise for the sake of a creed,*
  Or riot in hope of spoil,
  Equally will I punish the deed,
  Equally check the broil;

[69]

Nowise permitting injustice at all
From whatever doctrine it springs —
But — whether ye follow Priapus or Paul,
I care for none of these things."

These words of Kipling (from " Gallio's Song "), and the authorized translation from the Scripture do the Roman injustice; the passage really means: Gallio felt that the accusation was not in his jurisdiction to handle.

And yet, even though Seneca may have known St. Paul, and although he embraced a Stoicism which was in general nearer to Christianity than the Stoicism of any predecessor, it was, in particular, his view of humanity that drew the interest of the Church,— a sympathy with his fellow-men. We have no record of any legislation originated by him which showed a desire to repress or torment mankind. He was an apostle of humanitarianism.

Although we know that the Greeks frequently felt scruples as to the advisability of slavery, we know that reform never came and that " big business " and the slave trade at Delos were too strong for the sentimentalists. Roman law treated the slave as a *res*, and the

[70]

early Romans gave the law every benefit when in doubt. After Augustus came a reign of terror, manifesting itself in family rather than in national rebellions. Textbooks on Roman law show us that by the time of Vespasian many acts had been passed for the protection of the slave; also that the Antonines improved matters still more. And by the time of Justinian the slave question was no longer an issue. Two letters of Seneca (47 and 70) represent the philosopher as protesting against current custom: " I am glad to hear, Lucilius, that you live on friendly terms with your slaves; . . . they are our friends, nay, rather, our fellow-slaves, because Fortune has power over us no less than over *them*. . . . Let them speak freely in your presence, so that they may not gossip behind your back. . . . Do not subject them to humiliating tasks. Let them *dine in company with you*. . . . Assume that your coachman is a gentleman, and you will make him one! " Seneca's practice evidently conformed to his precept, since he allows (83.4) his pace-maker to chaff him on his " second childhood." And among the many heroes who met death voluntarily, in addition to the Catos and admirals and generals, there was a poor Doric slave-boy who dashed his head against a wall, and a German gladiator who discovered a grewsome method of exit from the sordid barracks where he was incarcerated. These bits of protest are not limited to Seneca; but we may sum up his revolt on the serf question by contrasting him with such genial writers as the Younger Pliny, who treat their slaves like spoiled children, and go comfortably about their business. Even Epictetus reflects this tendency. Seneca is the most outspoken of all.

Feminism, that most modern of all modern topics, offers the most fruitful field for Seneca's reform ideas. As the Eternal City became more cosmopolitan, woman took a prominent part as *dominatrix* of the salon, as did her successor in eighteenth century France. The result of it all in high life was a sort of cynical compromise in her relations with man; Seneca, although he had burned his fingers in court intrigue, seems to have been happy in his two marriages. And in his writings he takes higher ground than one would expect in high life during such an epoch. His death and the circumstances of his death speak volumes; so does the 104th Letter:

[72]

" I went into the country for a change of air, despite the reluctance of my dear Paulina; I quoted my brother Gallio's words — that disease is a matter of place and not of constitution — for Paulina is always recommending me to guard my health. Since I know that our souls are united, I take care of her by taking care of myself. . . . A man who does not hold his wife . . . in high enough esteem to remain a little longer in this world for her sake, is an effeminate laggard." " What is sweeter than to be so loved by one's wife that one is dearer to one's own self for this very reason? "

In the abstract, we find several statements of a new viewpoint. For example: " How unreasonable it is for a man to insist on conjugal fidelity in his wife, and at the same time to be in love with the wives of other men! " Seneca far outdistances other Roman writers in his championing of women; Marcus Aurelius, with sad eyes, says little, for he was Faustina's husband. Epictetus regards a wife and children as so much baggage which must be faithfully checked. Cicero regards women, (including the cross-grained and rheumatic Terentia) as necessary evils, excepting, of course, his daughter Tullia. Even Pliny, with his charming description of a Roman girl, with his shrewd understanding of middle-aged ladies (including his mother-in-law), and with his kindness in securing husbands for young girls whose provinciality has perhaps scared off suitors, takes us into a world which resembles " Cranford," where no one does anything unusual. But Seneca burns with modern ideas. Scribonia jests in the face of probable execution, when called into council by a scapegrace nephew. " Why trouble yourself," says the excellent lady, " with doing what others will do for you? " Seneca also mentions the famous case of Sattia, a sort of female Old Parr in Roman legend. Sattia was a noblewoman who lived in the reign of Claudius and whose physician left orders to carve on his tomb the fact that he had doctored the withered dame almost to the bourne of a hundred years. " You see that some persons actually boast about their age. Now who could have endured the old lady's remarks, had she lived to complete her century of existence? "

These are cases from the aristocracy. But the wide sympathy of Seneca is proved by his sympathetic account of the slave-woman Harpasté. " You are aware, of course, my dear

Lucilius, that Harpasté, my wife's female clown, has been retained in my household as a burden from a legacy. Personally, I hate all these freaks; whenever I wish to enjoy the quips of a fool, I have not far to seek; I can laugh at myself. Be that as it may, my fool suddenly lost her eyesight. The story sounds incredible, but it is true; she doesn't know that she is blind. She keeps asking her attendant to change her quarters, says that the house is too dark. Now what amuses us in the case of Harpasté clearly happens to all the rest of us; . . . the blind seek a guide, but we wander guideless and seek excuses."

There is on the one side a serious appeal for the rights of woman, and on the other a half humorous understanding of feminine fancy. Perhaps the facts can be explained by some wondrous mother-influence (and there is evidence in Seneca's other works to support this theory), such as we find in the *Muetterchen* of Goethe.

Another outspoken word is that which deals with the gladiator-athlete. Cicero is intellectually bored with the games, and so is Pliny; but Seneca roundly denounces the " bleacherite." " Those who are beefy in body are beefy in brains." "There is nothing worse than large quantities of wine poured into a stomach fatigued from heavy exercise." Instead of boxing and wrestling, he says, try jumping, cross-country running, and dumb-bell exercises. "An educated man is a fool to be always thinking of enlarging his biceps; . . . try as you will, you can never grow to be as strong as a first-class bull." "If a man's body can be toughened in the choking dust and under the blinding sun, why cannot the mind also be trained by plain living and high thinking? " This devotion to brainless brawn befits, he declares, neither the scholar nor the gentleman; how wise was that gladiator who, on the way to the morning exhibition, inserted his head beween the chariot spokes and won his release! Avoid crowds! They defile you. " The other day I went to a show; it was pure manslaughter instead of the rest and relaxation which I expected. ' Kill him, lash him, brand him! ' cried the mob; . . . ' Why doesn't he die game? ' . . . Do you not suppose that evil sights like these return to plague him who beholds them? " *Panem et circenses!*

The eighty-third letter is devoted to denouncing alcoholism. We note with amusement how Seneca characteristically begins with a syllogism of Zeno: " No one entrusts a secret to a drunken man; but one will entrust a secret to a good man; therefore the good man will not get drunk " ; and how he ridicules this logic by framing the absurd: " No one entrusts a secret to a man asleep; but one will entrust a secret to a good man; therefore the good man does not go to sleep." He concludes that it is better to " arraign drunkenness frankly and to expose its vices . . . show that drunkenness is nothing but a condition of insanity purposely assumed. . . . Explain by facts, and not mere words, the revolting aspect of the habit, and its haunting evils." Seneca was all his life a teetotaller.

We have thus seen [12] how far thought and human sympathy have progressed in the mind of Seneca, as contrasted with Aristotle, who deemed a slave to be a machine, a woman to be a passive link between two generations, and the habits of man in general to be controlled by the scheme of the state rather than by the will of the individual. It is this cumulative process of progressive interest in his fellow-men that makes Seneca attractive in the eyes of Chaucer, Thomas à Kempis, and Emerson. His love for mankind was a creed rather than a platform.

Before proceeding to outline further the influence of this versatile Spanish Roman upon later generations, I shall quote his famous lines [13] upon the joy of reading: "The only men in the world who are really at leisure, and really living, are those devoted to the study of wisdom. Indeed, they are not only guardians of their own careers, but they are adding all eternity to their store; whatever years have gone before them, are to be counted as their property. And unless we are most unappreciative, those noble pioneers in high thinking were born for our benefit and fashioned their lives for our sakes. We are brought to consider things of the greatest worth which have been dug up from darkness into daylight by the effort of others; to no period of history are we forbidden access, and we are admitted everywhere. If by greatness of soul we may pass beyond the narrow confines of human frailty, we have unlimited time through which we may course. We may share in the thoughts of all philosophers. And since the universe allows us to go into partnership with all the ages, why, in this tiny and fleeting state of transition should we not give ourselves whole-heartedly to the things which are unbounded, eternal, and to be shared with our betters? . . . Shall we not say that men are engaged upon real duties who wish to be on the most inti-mate terms with the thinkers of past ages? Every one of these will give you his attention; every one of these will send you away happier and more devoted; no one of them will allow you to depart empty-handed from his presence. They can be found by night or by day, and by anyone who wishes.

"None of them will compel you to die, and yet all of them can teach you how to die. None will wear your life out, but will give their own lives to you. It will not harm you to chat with them, nor will their friendship mean death to you or their association expense to you. Gifts they will give you,— whatever you will; they will not be responsible for your satisfaction being less than your craving. What happiness and what a noble old age abides for one who has given himself into their patronage! He will have friends with whom to converse on things small or great, whom he may call into council daily, from whom he may hear the truth without insult, praise without flattery, according to whose image he may pattern himself.

" These souls will show you the path to immortality and will raise you to heights from which no one is cast down. . . . Anything will be destroyed by the flight of time; but harm can never come to that which wisdom has hallowed."

How much like Southey's

> " The mighty minds of old,
>   My never-failing friends are they,
>   With whom I converse day by day!"

It is therefore on grounds of great sympathy, as well as through resemblance to Christian sentiments, that the church embraced Seneca. He had approached the theme of sin and suffering and righteousness in a more human spirit than Cicero's sages or indeed than any leader of previous pagan philosophy and religion, save only Socrates.

IV. HOW HE TOUCHED THE MEDIEVAL MIND

CHRISTIANITY, therefore, placed Seneca on a firmer foundation. He had caught up with the currents of thought which his Roman contemporaries found foreign to their ideals. With this tradition of respect there is now intermingled the admiration of medieval scholars, theologians, and people of affairs. And be it remembered that most of the people of affairs in these centuries were churchmen. The prevalence of ninth and tenth century manuscripts of Seneca alone would indicate special interest throughout this period,— in addition to the commonplace books called " Seneks " which we shall see later cropping out in Chaucer. The name " Senek " is formed on the analogy of the grammars known as "Donets " (Donatus), named from the first authority who wrote on the subject. We find also " *Monita*," " *Libri de Moribus*," " *Senecae proverbia*," — gathered, in several cases, before the eighth century and serving for many a medieval quotation, often without acknowledgment. They become typical " hand-me-downs " of a proverbial nature,— accretions like a collection of ballads or like a Joe-Miller jest-book or the Till Eulenspiegel literature in Germany.

Seneca thus becomes no less honored for his literary qualities than for his spiritual inspiration. Hildebert, writing to Henry I, mentions him; Gerbert, in the tenth century, refers to him; the correspondence between Abelard and Heloise opens with the famous saying of our philosopher: " You must not limit your study of philosophy to your leisure moments " ; and Alanus de Insulis,[14] that purple patcher of homily and imagery, lineal descendant of Martianus Capella and the school of allegory, is replete with Seneca's words and thoughts. Alanus combines the pagan allegory with the ingredients of Christianity, as Seneca himself puts a touch of mystic monotheism into the Stoic framework; coming together from opposite directions they reach the same point of view. Wisdom is invoked in the Senecan manner; Epictetus and Aurelius have less of the medieval touch. The four pagan virtues are enlarged by the addition of

Chastity and Generosity and others of the goodly galaxy whom we see playing a part in great literature down through Spenser's *Faerie Queene*. The *De Planctu Naturae* is full of " the transgression of the earthly sphere, the disorders in the ordering of the world, the carelessness of government, the unjustness of law," — harangues resembling the passages on mundane sin which fill the *Epistles* and the *Natural History* of Seneca. " The world grows worse, and now its golden age departs " ; " the wretch has nothing when he thinks that he has nothing, since his longings balance his riches with poverty." " By this pest and plague of flattery are smitten those . . . who offer lulling praises to the hearing of prelates; who either shake from the coats of such men a fictitious dust, or pretend to pick a feather off a featherless garment." " There Cato was intoxicated with the golden nectar of virtuous sobriety; Plato shone with the sidereal splendor of genius." The style and the thoughts here given show how little the " point " of Silver Latin rhetoric had lost its sting, and how near in sympathy these Christian scholars were to the author of the words: " Avarice . . . made all things the property of others, and reduced itself from boundless wealth to straitened need. It was avarice that introduced poverty and, by craving much, lost all."

The *Naturales Quaestiones* becomes the standard work of the Middle Ages on tides, earthquakes, and comets; it is the more advanced counterpart of the *Physiologi*,— the schoolbooks on obvious animal life which pointed a moral for convent classes. John Scotus Erigena, Amaury of Béne, Otto of Freising, Giraldus Cambrensis, and Peter of Blois, all refer to Seneca as scientist and philosopher. So does Vincent of Beauvais,[15] in many passages of his *Mirror of Nature.*

Giraldus the Welshman invokes him, especially in the *Itinerary Through Wales.* In the third chapter he is attacking the Cistercians who degenerated into luxurious ways. " As Seneca says, ' Too great happiness makes men greedy, nor are their desires ever so temperate as to terminate in what is acquired.' " And in the fifth chapter likewise: " Seneca says, ' He falls not badly who rises stronger from his fall,' "—with reference to the humbling and subsequent promotion of an abbot. Again, " Hence the observation of Seneca that the malicious attention of the envious reader dwells with no less satisfaction on a faulty than on an elegant expression, and is as anxious to discover what it may ridicule as what it may commend." Bernard of Clairvaux takes from the 20th *Epistle* a motto for the Crusades: " When this throng shall cease being fed by thee, it will feed itself . . . the forsakers of the throng will be those who followed, not thee, but some other guiding star." Bernard is simply continuing the policy set by the Church, of amalgamating its own thought-processes with those of such predecessors as this Empire philosopher; the other writers mentioned are touched by his philosophic and literary appeal.

The wizards also follow Seneca. Roger Bacon, master of the thirteenth century, while speculating in his *Opus Majus* on geography, harks back to the *Naturales Quaestiones* as " repeating Aristotle's ideas of the proximity of Spain and India." Bacon regards him as peer among classical authors; he quotes him often. And he records a search for his works, carried on for twenty years, amid forbidding surroundings, together with those of " Aristotle, Avicenna, Cicero, and other ancients," whose writings are no less difficult to purchase.

[85]

John of Salisbury adopts the proverb of the Pinching Shoe, which branches off from Seneca's *De Matrimonio* through Jerome. And he also comes to the defence of Seneca in answer to Quintilian: "If Quintilian will excuse my saying so, there are very few, if any, writers on conduct among non-Christians whose words and ideas can be more readily applied to all kinds of practical things." [16]

Grosseteste,[17] the contemporary of Bacon, quotes away; but anyone can quote; Grosseteste stands out interestingly as the author of Christian phrase-books modelled on the Roman; they are *Dicta*, with sub-topics such as *Patience*,— the Christian counterpart of all the moralizing which made Seneca so popular during this era. Grosseteste remarks also that he hesitated about journeying to Rome, but that he went ahead because he refused to be numbered with men who are " tossed about with every wind of doctrine," or " with the swimmers of whom Seneca says that they are carried along by the current." It is also interesting to note that Johannes de Garlandia in a literary history (13th century) includes Seneca among the Latin authors to be read. These admirers of his knew him as the

[86]

writer of the *Epistles, Naturales Quaestiones, De Beneficiis, Tragedies,* and the *Declamations,* wrongly ascribing the Elder Seneca's work on rhetoric to the son. It was not until Raphael of Volaterra and Lipsius that this error was rectified. These names are among the most important of their time, and we may properly, before reaching Dante, close with a comparison made by Thomas Aquinas, who couples Seneca's " it is indeed excess to know more than one needs " with Augustine's " overdone craving is cloaked under the name of learning and science." But measure was never a virtue in the Middle Ages.

V. HOW THE RENAISSANCE
VIEWED HIM

DID DANTE, having all the *Flori-legia* and *Dicta Philosophorum* at his command, go to the original works of Seneca, preferring, with his penetrating intellect, not to trust to such " elegant extracts " ? It is safe to agree with Professor E. Moore [18] that he did so. Dante's temperament was not one that took things at second hand.

In the First Circle of the Inferno were " souls with sedate and placid eyes," " glorious spirits in august array," and among them were the Greek heroes and philosophers,

> " *With Orpheus, Zeno, and Hippocrates,*
> *Tullius, Linus, Seneca —* "

men who are shut out from perfect rewards only through the lack of Christianity. This is their sole bar to complete immortality; and Dante shows himself perhaps even stricter in this regard than the Fathers of the Church. Seneca's *Letters* are the medium of his renown, and it is through them that he is chiefly known during this period. Dante quotes or clearly reflects Seneca more than a dozen times; and sometimes even improves upon his original in force and point. His scholarship is fairly accurate; there existed even in his day a learned doubt as to the identity of Seneca the Moralist and Seneca the Tragic Poet.

In the *Convito* occur the words: "perche dice Seneca: ' che nulla cosa più cara si compera, che quella dove i prieghi si spendono,' " — a frequent theme in the Latin philosopher, as in the famous tenth satire of Juvenal. In the 76th *Letter* Seneca advises men to keep on learning " as long as they are ignorant, or, in the words of the proverb, as long as they are alive," — which Dante abbreviates incisively to: " Se l' uno de' piedi avessi nel sepolcro, apprendere vorrei." Yet a saying of the Jurist Salvius Julianus keeps the " foot-in-the-grave " metaphor more closely than Seneca's proverb. Dante also has a fellow-feeling with Seneca regarding the ostentation of riches: "quanto contra richezza Seneca, massimamente a Lucillo scrivendo," — which is reflected from many a harangue in the *Epistles* and the *Natural History*. Finally, Dante has a passage on meteors from the *Natural History,* perhaps filtered through the work of Albertus Magnus.

As Dante did a service to Seneca's memory in Italy, so Chaucer established him as a literary and philosophical authority in England. Chaucer's classical affiliations have been carefully studied; we know that he brought Virgil and Ovid and Statius and Boethius into the limelight of cultivated England. With them came Seneca; but from what sources? Was it from "Seneks" or commonplace books? Was it direct from manuscripts? Or was it from a combination of the two?

Piers Plowman, in upholding communism as a panacea, "proves it by Seneca." Professor Ayres is justified in assuming a much greater influence than mere "elegant extracts" such as those which we have mentioned above. And it is significant that by his time the spurious Pauline correspondence seems to be making less and less of an impression.

Chaucer [19] refers to "Senecciens" as well as to "Seneks." These followers, or members of a school, or modern lovers of Seneca are mentioned in the *Boece:* " The Senecciens and the Canios and the Sorans, of which folke the renown is neither over-olde ne unsolempne." As Seneca had his Cato-cult,— the worship of the typical Roman Stoic hero,— so later generations seem to have developed a Seneca-cult.

The Monk's Tale contains an extended account of Nero's tutordom at the hands of Seneca:

" In *yowthe a maister hadde this emperour,*
  To teche hym letterure and curteysie,—
  For of moralitee he was the flour,
  As *in his tyme, but if bookes lye;*

  .   .   .   .

  This Seneca, of which that I devyse,
  By-cause that Nero hadde of him swich drede,
  For he fro vices wolde hym ay chastise
  Discreetly, as by word, and nat by dede;
  ' Sire,' wolde he seyn, ' an emperour moot nede
  Be vertuous and hate tirannye;'
  For which he in a bath made hym to blede
  On both his armes, til he moste dye."

It is thus a literary as well as a historical commonplace that the *Ministre Malgré Lui* should be hailed as the classical example of ruling under difficulties and of controlling the many-headed beast of Imperial Rome. Calvin's commentary, for example, on Seneca's *De Clementia* in 1532 reflects the attempt on the part of a thoughtful scholar to influence a monarch towards tolerance (in this case of the Protestants); and the whole career, with many of his speeches and sermons, of Bossuet, was an endeavor to create in the Dauphin an attitude of clemency towards those in lower places and in higher realms of thought. The proverbial philosopher-king thus came near becoming historic fact; and the ideal of Seneca manifested itself in later generations. It is also significant of the Roman's prominence at this time that in Chaucer's *Parson's Tale* our philosopher is classed with Augustine, Solomon, and St. Paul.

The *Melibeus* predominates in references from Seneca, even though Albertanus of Brescia is the middleman for their circulation. The Latin original, dating from the thirteenth century, may or may not have been Chaucer's source; at all events, we find therein about twenty saws which go back to Seneca — the larger portion from the 63rd *Letter*. Perhaps less than half of them are direct, all the others deriving from some commonplace book. It is noteworthy that Albertanus' genuine loans are drawn from the *Epistles*.

A passage in the *Parson's Tale* (I. 759): " And therefore seith Seneca: ' thy prudence sholde live benignly with thy thralles,' " may be compared to the kernel of the 47th *Letter: familiariter te cum servis vivere.* The whole Chaucerian theme is so consecutive, when laid alongside the Latin, that steady reading in the original seems to have taken place, rather than mere picking out of isolated topics from a handbook of extracts.

The Pardoner, that winning rascal, discourses most eloquently against drunkenness and gluttony: (c. 492ff):

" *Senek seith eke a good word douteless;*
 He seith he can no difference fynde
 Betwix a man that is out of his mynde
 And a man which that is dronkelewe;
 But that woodnesse, fallen in a shrewe,
 Persevereth lenger than doth dronkennesse."

This may be laid alongside a passage from the 83rd *Letter*: " To be drunk is nothing else than to be crazy on purpose; for if you continue the habit of intoxication for several days, can you entertain any doubt about your madness? Even now, it is shorter, but not any less intense."

> " Thise cokes, how they stampe, and streyne, and
>   grinde,
>   And turnen substance into accident,
>   To fulfille al thy likerous talent!"

may be directly taken from Seneca's " Behold these kitchens of ours, with the cooks bustling about from stove to stove! Do you think that it can be for one stomach alone that this food is being prepared with so much turmoil? " Again, it must have been from more than a mere book of sayings that the Man of Law (B 20–28) derived his remarks on Time:

> " Wel can Senek, and many a philosophre
>   Bewailen tyme, more than gold in cofre.
>   ' For los of catel may recovered be,
>   But los of tyme shendeth us,' quod he."

For this, Chaucer must have read consecutively in the first *Epistle*, which says: " So great is the folly of mankind, that they allow the cheapest and most useless things, which can easily be replaced, to be charged in the reckoning, . . . but they never regard themselves as in debt when they have received some of that precious commodity, time! "

Finally, the *Canterbury Tales* afford us one more direct and clear comparison, in the Wife of Bath's remarks upon the simple life:

" G*lad poverte is an honest thing, certeyn;*
 T*hus wol Senek and other clerkes sayn.*
 W*hoso that halt him payd of his poverte,*
 I *holde him riche, al had he nat a sherte.*
 He *that coveyteth is a poor wight,*
 F*or he wolde have that is not in his might.*
 B*ut he that noghte hath, ne coveyteth have,*
 I*s riche, al-though ye holde him but a knave.*"
  (D. 1183–90)

This follows without question the thought of the second *Letter:* " Glad poverty is an honorable estate, says Epicurus. Now it is not poverty if it is glad. For the man of poverty is one who craves too much, rather than one who has too little."

There remains the *Troilus,* with its shrewd moralizing and its well-sutured anachronisms. Boccaccio's Pandaro is converted into Chaucer's Pandarus by the aid of many wise saws from Seneca, unacknowledged, as is the case throughout the *Troilus.*

" And witeth wel, that bothe two ben vyces,
　Mistrusten alle, or elles alle leve " (I. 687)

has its origin in *Epistle* III: " both are vices,
trusting everyone and trusting no one." Again,

　" Delyte not in wo thy wo to seche," (I. 704)

echoes from the 99th *Epistle:* " What is more
shameful than to catch at pleasure in the very
midst of pain.'" Compare also

" For certeinly, the first poynt is this
　Of noble courage and of wel ordeyne,
　A man to have pees with himself, y-wis; "

and (Ep. 2.1) " The first proof of a well-
ordered mind is to be able to pause and linger
within itself."

We are perhaps back again in the commonplace book atmosphere when we compare short
bits like

" He that parted is in evry place
　Is no-wher hool, as writen clerkes wyse " (I. 960),

with the neat " everywhere means nowhere "
of the second *Letter,* or even when the passage
on the inadvisability of transplanting (I. 964)

is set alongside of " A plant which is often moved can never grow strong " (Ep. 2.3).

In all these cases we are on delicate ground if we insist on direct connection with the works of Seneca. We must remember, for example, that the *Physician's Tale* came to Chaucer from Livy through the *Romaunt of the Rose,* that the handbooks were full of " Seneks," and that many a continental author like Albertanus of Brescia served as a clearing-house for the English master, as he did for others. But we possess enough of a residuum to decide, with Professor Ayres, that Seneca must have, in certain parts at least, been familiar to Chaucer *per se* and in his own works.

Dante, then, had a bowing acquaintance with Seneca; Chaucer used him still more; but Petrarch,[20] the guide-post of the Renaissance, the " first modern man," the pioneer humanist to whom all the literary tribe are so deeply in debt, made him a very part of his mind and soul. Seneca comes second only to Virgil in the number of quotations. The first library at Vaucluse contained two copies of *Ad Lucillium*. The catalogue of the library, too, drew its motto from the second *Epistle* of Seneca:

" non transfuga sed explorator transire soleo,"
to which Petrarch prefixed his own phrase:
" peculiares ad religionem." Again, Petrarch's
epistolary style was modelled upon that of
Seneca rather than upon that of Cicero; since
the works of the latter did not come into his
ken until his forty-first year, and by that
time his style was formed. Pliny, of course,
was a sealed book to him. Petrarch wished
to leave behind him a collection of letters
resembling the Latin master's or such as those
of Abelard. Many of Petrarch's letters are
built like Seneca's, and so it is with the essays
also. In the *De Remediis,* the architecture
is in many instances parallel: the essay opens
with such concrete description as that of the
palaestra, and goes on to draw the moral,—
how much better it is not to contend for
human prizes, but for the Great Olympic of
Life. Petrarch, as he grows older, inclines
towards Cicero: " I recollect that Seneca
laughed at Cicero for including trivial matters
in his letters, and yet I am much more prone
in my epistles to follow Cicero's example than
Seneca's. Seneca, indeed, gathered into his
letters pretty much all the moral reflections
which he had published in his various books;

Cicero, on the other hand, treats philosophical subjects in his books, but fills his letters with miscellaneous news and the gossip of the day. Let Seneca think as he likes about this; as for me, I must confess that I find Cicero's letters very agreeable reading. They relax the tension produced by weighty matters." This is true; but Petrarch's *Epistles*, which are, like Seneca's own, carefully elaborated essays, do not resemble the fact-packed correspondence of the master of Roman oratory so much as the discourses of Seneca to Lucilius,— each revolving about a point, and each concentrated until the subject is exhausted.

We may prove this by quoting at length a passage from Petrarch's *De Remediis Utriusque Fortunae* (II. 29) on Slaves: " nota sunt . . . hac in re Senecae consilia,— vivendum cum servis familiariter, comiter, clementer: familiarem esse iubet . . . addit non verberum sed verborum castigatione utendum . . . admittendos praeterea in sermonem, in consilium, in convictum, . . . in servo verum opinatur quod iam ante de amico dixerat. Fidelem si credideris, facies."

In a Letter to Seneca, furthermore, he shows that the content, as well as the style, of that author was peculiarly congenial to him: " In one department of learning, however, he did not blush to acknowledge that the genius of the Greeks was distinctly inferior, saying that he knew not whom to place on a par with thee in the field of moral philosophy." Quotations are so numerous that it is futile and pedantic to heap them up. Petrarch's love for Seneca is proved most conclusively of all by his recording in his copy of Virgil along with the date of Laura's death, the passage from the 86th *Epistle:* " the soul of her, as Seneca says of Africanus, I am fully persuaded to have returned to the heaven whence it came." Petrarch thus enshrouds in a passage from a well-loved author the memory of his own best-beloved.

Perhaps the clearest proof of all that our philosopher made a fundamental appeal to the Middle Ages and the early Renaissance is the fact that the University of Piacenza possessed a Professor of Seneca! This put him on a par with the study of Aristotle at the University of Paris.

Thomas à Kempis, that wondrously elusive and haunting mystic whose *Imitation* has drawn the essence of the flower of quietism, refers at length to the 7th *Epistle* (" On Crowds "): " One saith: ' As oft as I have gone among men, I returned home less a man.' " It seems entirely possible that the author may have used the direct works of Seneca, instead of quoting " loosely, from a commonplace book," as Dr. Bigg, the editor, remarks. This inspired writer of Biblical centos has much in common with Seneca; a quietist himself, a practical reformer as well as leader in a professed denominational brotherhood, he has the same attitude towards the world's bustle and the distractions of mankind. . . . " Bear thyself as an exile and pilgrim upon earth . . . the habit and shaven crown do little profit; but change of manners and perfect mortification of passions make a true religious man " ; " I teach without fence of logic " ; "What have I to do with *genera* and *species?* " " In the morning purpose, and at night examine thy manners, how thou hast behaved thyself this day in word, deed, and thought; for in these perhaps thou hast often offended both God and thy neighbor." Identically such thoughts and musings, while not incontrovertibly Senecan, are found in the Latin philosopher. To a marked degree these two thinkers feel the "mystery of this unintelligible world."

Soon after this time begins the age of editions. Just as the ninth and tenth centuries were the heyday of MSS., so in 1475 began a far larger diffusion through the press. The first printed Seneca appeared at Naples in that year; the first edition is by Erasmus in 1515, followed by a second in 1529. Froude tells us that in October 1516, Erasmus "writes from Brussels to Peter Giles . . . in fraternal good humour, advising him to be regular at his work, to keep a journal, to remember that life was short, to study Plato and Seneca, love his wife, and disregard the world's opinion." The swift and pithy thoughts of Seneca always appealed to Erasmus: "The lynx can see farther than you can; the swans surpass you in colour and beauty, but only man can appreciate the pity of God." Calvin a few years later turned out a *De Clementia*. Pincianus produced another edition in 1536; and the climax of scholarly attention came with the monumental volumes of Lipsius in 1605 and the English translation by the Elizabethan Thomas Lodge in 1614. Golding in 1577 had translated the *De Beneficiis;* and Lipsius himself " made for a style founded on Tacitus and Seneca," — an innovation which caused some discussion in literary and scholarly circles. From the late 15th century, therefore, we may say that our philosopher circulated freely in Europe and that from this time onward his influence became much wider, cropping out in all sorts of unimagined places and under unexpected circumstances.

Alexander Barclay, who flourished at the beginning of the sixteenth century, perpetrated a translation of Sebastian Brandt's *Narrenschiff*, "The Ship of Fooles," a curious moralizing poem, typical in its character-drawing,— in which a sort of Theophrastian Noah's Ark is catalogued and described. Such diatribes as this by Barclay against luxury, replete with Seneca, Juvenal, Plutarch, Ovid, and other classical authors, had floated down the Middle Ages to the Renaissance on many an alien craft:

" *Where is Curius and abstynence soverayne,*
Where is old Persemony wont to be so gode?
Where is the old measure of mannys life and
        fode? "

[103]

In the course of the voyaging allusion is made to Seneca:

" So *Socrates, so Senyk, and Plato*
  Suffred great wrong, great iniury and payne;
  And of your faith sayntis right many mo
  For Christ our mayster did great turment
      sustayne."

And throughout are to be found such philosophical commonplaces as:

" *The wyse man to utter the trouthe is not aferde*
  Though he shoulde be closyd within the bull of
      bras
  Of Phalaris the tyrant."

Cato is one of the heroes and models; the work
of Seneca is as clear among the sources as is
that of Plutarch and other of the hero-
biographers.

VI. MONTAIGNE AND THE ELIZABETHANS

WE HAVE seen enough to draw a conclusion regarding the qualities of Seneca which appealed to pioneers in thought and in religion. The Roman moralist had been singled out by the early church as a pagan champion of Christianity; he was taken over by them as a kindred spirit, as one whose flexible catholicity pointed forward to ages unborn rather than backward to classical models. We note his appeal to Dante the medieval leader, to Chaucer the first modern Englishman, to Petrarch the apostle of humanism. And all this, much as it is, takes second place when compared with the way in which he is regarded by Montaigne, " the first person," as Hazlitt remarked, " who had the courage to say as an author what he felt as a man."

Michael de Montaigne [21] was preceded by a host of translators and commentators on Seneca, who left much material and much interest ready to his hand. Rabelais' Gargantua read "Sénèque de IV Virtutibus" with his tutor, though we know now that this book was a collection of Senecan ideas by Martinus Dumiensis, of the sixth century. Charron, author of the *Sagesse,* declares: "I have taken the greater part of the material for this work from the best authors who have treated this subject of morals and politics, which is the true science of man, as well ancient, especially the great doctors Seneca and Plutarch, as modern." Geoffrey de la Chassaigne, Montaigne's brother-in-law, had made a translation of Seneca. In fact, his name was so widely known that when Pasquier desires to praise the essays of Montaigne he does it in this wise: "As for his essays, which I call masterpieces, there is no book which I have so greatly cherished. I always find something in it to please me. 'Tis a French Seneca." And finally, we have a well-drawn picture of the tragedy-smitten D'Aubigné in *Les Tragiques,* who is represented as deeply impressed by the deaths of Seneca and Thrasea. The days, then, of the court of Henry of Navarre lent themselves to this cult.

We are so familiar with the grand Sieur

Eyquem that it is almost superfluous to refer to his genial declaration of theft: "I never seriously settled myself to the reading of any book of solid learning, but Plutarch and Seneca; and then, like the Danaides, I eternally fill, and it constantly runs out." Or, "la science que j'y cherche y est traictée à pièces discousues." "Such are the minor works of the first, and the *Epistles* of the latter, which are the best and most profitable of all their writings." "Seneca is more various and undulating, more proper for private sanction and more firm." Montaigne's titles are suggestive; the *Essay of Books* quotes Ep. 90: utrum peccare aliquis nolit; Ep. 103: licet sapere sine pompa; Ep. 33: non sumus sub rege; Ep. 88 and Ep. 106.

All these Frenchmen, and especially Montaigne, found Seneca congenial because he was not limited to philosophical definitions in support of a single school or a single end, because he was not writing a text-book of Greek philosophy for Roman readers, because he was not consciously polishing up a correspondence which should serve later as a mirror for a certain epoch of Roman history. He wrote for the world. Montaigne's world had become over-courtly; the era of jeweled swords was to give way to the era of adventurous exploration both in geography and in thought. And this interesting French literary Cervantes, this upsetter of tradition, sought and found in the moralist of the early Roman Empire a kindred spirit. These men served no masters. They took all humanity to be their province.

Plutarch permeated England through the translation of Sir Thomas North; and Seneca reached the British vernacular by means of Thomas Lodge. But before those days, and since those days also, many men had him at their tongues' and pens' end. Elyot, in the *Governour,* cites him often. Ascham, a Ciceronian, debates " whether one or many are to be followed; and if one, who is that one — Seneca or Cicero; Sallust or Caesar." Sir Thomas Wyat's *Epigrams* are full of Seneca. Henry Parker, Lord Morley, *To his Posterity,* sings:

" The *mind out of quiet,"* so sage Seneca saith,
" It *had been no felicity, but a painful death."*

Turberville, *The Lover of Cupid for Mercie,* says of the various sages who uphold reason and decry love:

> " Next *Plutarch Senec came,*
> *Severe in all his sawes,*
> *Who cleane defide your wanton tricks*
> *And scornde your childish lawes.*"

Wyat's *Renouncing of Love* contains the lines:

> " Farewell love, and all thy lawes for ever;
> *Thy bayted hookes shall tangle me no more;*
> *Senec and Plato call me to their lore*
> *To parfit welth, my wit for to endever.*"

Thus early English poetry,— Renaissance and Elizabethan. We might multiply instances. Here Seneca is the prop for serious thinkers, the defense against a light-o'-love. Bishop Hall, who knew full well both these aspects of his fascinating London, was called the " Christian Seneca " from the " pith and clear sententiousness of his prose style " as well as from the weight of his serious utterances. We shall see later how this is borne out in the writings of Jeremy Taylor. The maintenance of this interest at a slightly earlier period, and the proof that men were dwelling on these problems, appears, for example, from the fact that in 1648 Sir Edward Sherborne translated " Seneca's answer to Lucilius' question: ' Why good men suffer Misfortunes, seeing there is a Divine Providence.' "

Random quotations, mostly unacknowledged, are frequent. Euphues ascribes to Seneca Plutarch's "Too much bending breaketh the bow." The Earl of Stirling refers to the dictum on pain (*si longus levis, si gravis brevis*) in his 63rd Sonnet:

" Oft *have I heard, which now I must deny,*
  T*hat nought can last if that it be extreme.*"

Donne, as usual, loads much philosophy into his lyrics:

  " Good *we must love, and must hate ill,*
    F*or ill is ill, and good good still;*
    B*ut there are things indifferent,*
    W*hich we may neither hate nor love,*
    B*ut one, and then another prove,*
    As *we shall find our fancy bent.*"

And Daniel quotes Seneca, in his *Defence of Rhyme.*

Ben Jonson,[22] a regular Senecan, had evidently been exploring in the *Naturales Quaestiones:*

" *Was she gracious a-farre off?   But neere*
  A terrour?   Or is all this but my feare?
  That as the water makes things, put in't streight,
  Crooked appeare; so that doth my conceipt."

In the *Underwoods* Jonson versifies much of
the *De Beneficiis*. He cannot write a lyric
without using some Latin passage:

  " *And as a cunning painter takes*
    In any curious peece you see,
    More pleasure while the thing he makes
    Then when 'tis made, why, so will we."

And Jonson's critical comment (*On Abrupt-
ness of Style*), similarly, runs back to Seneca:
" This is the fault of some Latin writers, within
these last hundred years, of my reading, and
perhaps Seneca may be appeacht of it; I accuse him not."

"To descend to those extreme anxieties and
foolish cavils of grammarians is able to break
a wit in pieces; being a work of manifold
misery and vainenesse to be *elementarii senes*."

Shakespeare, who blends everything into
himself, ill rewards any search for quotations.
His chief classical model was North's *Plutarch;*
and yet it is as futile to dissect him as it would

be to take to pieces a statue of Michelangelo.
All that we can do is wonder whether his omniv-
orous mind had hovered for a moment on a
passage of Stoic commonplace when he elevated
a simple thought (the saying: *patria est ubi-
cumque vales*) into language like this:

> " *All places that the eye of heaven visits
> Are to a wise man ports and happy havens,*" —

and then veto any idea of borrowing on the
part of Shakespeare!

There are but two places which seem to
show obligation. The disguised Duke, moralizing to Claudio in *Measure for Measure,*
undoubtedly harks back to Seneca, as well as
Claudio himself, who invokes death in Stoic
terms:

> " To *lie in cold obstruction and to rot;
> This sensible warm motion to become
> A kneaded clod; and the delighted spirit
> To bathe in fiery floods, or to reside
> In thrilling region of thick-ribbéd ice;
> To be imprisoned in the viewless winds,
> And blown in restless violence round about
> The pendent world;* " . . .

For the second passage, an extended study has been made by Sonnenschein of the " Quality of Mercy " speech in the *Merchant of Venice*. The writer compares in detail certain passages of Seneca's *De Clementia*, stating that " Shakespeare brings at the outset into clearer relief than professed political philosophers the saving quality of mercy in the rulers of men." Compare Portia's

> " It *becomes*
> *The* thronéd *monarch better than his crown*,"

with the " *nullum tamen clementia ex omnibus magis quam regem aut principem decet* " of *De Clementia* I, 3.3.

VII. THE MODERN VIEW: FROM BACON TO THE TWENTIETH CENTURY

FRANCIS BACON [23] has been compared to Seneca, by Canon Farrar. How fair such a juxtaposition may be admits of considerable doubt; but the omniscient qualities of the two minds, especially with regard to science, and an open-mindedness toward all philosophy might tempt us to agree partially with this statement. Bacon is redolent of Seneca; but he is so redolent of almost every classical author that it would be futile to single out Seneca for quotation. Suffice it to say that Seneca occurs equally often with any of the ancients. Bacon was the first critic to understand that the *Epistles* of Seneca are really essays. In the dedication of his own volume to Prince Henry, he calls them " essaies, dispersed meditaciouns, thoughe conveyed in the form of Epistles." Just as he gave Seneca credit for the creation of an important literary type, so he balances the account by criticizing him, along with Plato, Plutarch and Cicero, for having " spoiled the stricter investigation of truth." Bacon's very scientific point of view rebelled against monism, and dialectic, and any philosophy based upon form, in the same manner as William James, pluralistically and pragmatically inclined, rejects the absolutism, the " idealistic pantheism " of his nineteenth century predecessors. Bacon's was the laboratory method. And yet he concedes the inspiring qualities of these men: " It is a thing not hastily to be condemned: to clothe and adorn the obscurity even of philosophy itself with sensible and plausible elocution." He is full of detailed references to Seneca, understanding his acumen and analyzing his conclusions. "To seek to extinguish anger utterly is but a bravery of the Stoics. We have better oracles: ' Be angry but sin not; Let not the sun go down upon your anger.' "

There is almost an uncanny sense of fitness in the justice of Bacon's comments. For example, after entirely approving Seneca's political career, " to the eternal glory of learned governors," we note these words: " Seneca, who was condemned for many corruptions and crimes, and banished into a solitary island, kept a mean; and though his pen did not freeeze, yet he abstained from intruding into matters of business; but spent his time in writing books of excellent argument and use for all ages; though he might have made better choice (sometimes) of his dedications " (as, for example, in the letter to Polybius from exile). He sympathizes with the Roman's condemnation of sophisms and mental juggling; he is at one with him in the desire to apply scientific tests to knowledge; and he cites him times without number to add weight to an aphorism or cap a climax.

Very significant is Bacon's understanding of the passage from Seneca's *Medea*, wherein the discovery of America was by some thought to be forecast:

> *Venient annis saecula seris,*
> *Quibus Oceanus vincula rerum*
> *Laxet et ingens pateat tellus*
> *Tethysque novos detegat orbes*
> *Nec sit terris ultima Thule.*

Columbus, Roger Bacon, and the Cardinal d'Ailly (whose work Columbus studied) knew of this passage; it proves that some semi-supernaturalism became associated with Seneca, assigning to him prophetic power, as was the case with Virgil. But it is thought that the lines refer to the Spain-India route and a possibility of developing it; the *Ultima Thule* may have turned men's minds westward. Bacon, in his *Essay of Prophesies*, simply remarks that the passage " ought to serve but for winter talk by the fireside."

Burton's *Anatomy of Melancholy*, with its curious " parts," " sections," " members," and " subsections," shows the great prevalence of the Roman moralist in seventeenth century England: even the " pretender to learning must have his sentences for company, some scatterings of Seneca and Tacitus." The references are mostly direct: " it was a chief caveat of Seneca, ' a wound can never be cured that hath several plasters.' " " Yet hear that divine Seneca: *aliud agere quam nihil,*— ' better to do to no end, than nothing.' "

Cowley's essay " On the dangers of an honest man in much company " reminds us of the seventh *Epistle On Crowds;* and in the essay " Of Myself," the self-effacing retirement so often advocated by the Roman is praised by the

Englishman. Cowley also (*Essay of Solitude*) quotes the eighty-sixth *Letter*, describing the retreat of Scipio at Liternum, as a sample of greatness avoiding the madding crowd. Herrick, curiously enough, weaves into his verse much of this philosophy, strange as it may seem to find a British Catullus moralizing. And Prior was so moved by the contemplation of Jordan's painting at the house of the Earl of Exeter that he produced a poem " On a Picture of Seneca dying in a Bath."

Finally, three English saints of the seventeenth century discovered in Seneca a kindred spirit: Jeremy Taylor, Thomas Trahearne, and Henry Vaughan. They found him a spiritual prop, as Montaigne found him a literary prop. Taylor interweaves pagan with Christian texts in his *Holy Living and Dying*, as follows: " Idleness is called the *sin of Sodom and her daughters,* and indeed is the burial of a living man, an idle person being so useless to any purposes of God and man, that he is like one that is dead, unconcerned in the changes and necessities of the world; and he only lives to spend his time, and eat the fruits of the earth." Or, " The Christian religion in all its moral parts is nothing else but the law of nature and great reason, complying with the great necessities of all the world." " Neither do thou get to thyself a private theatre of flatterers," quoting Ep. 7.9. Taylor is full of this non-Christian moralizing; he saw, as the Church Fathers saw long before him, that one can have no better advocate than an outsider who speaks the same language.

Henry Vaughan, *On Sir T. Bodley's Library*, sings:

> " *Rare Seneca! How lasting is thy breath!*
> *Though Nero did, thou couldst not bleed to death.*
> *How dull the expert Tyrant was, to look*
> *For that in thee, which livéd in thy Book!* "

also, " Patience: that which being made evil by abuse, yet in that state hath been commended by men that were not evil, by Seneca in his *Cato*. . . ."

And the curiously mystical Thomas Trahearne, who relies on Scripture and little besides for his literary furniture, remarks: " So that Seneca philosophized rightly when he said: ' Deus me dedit solum toti mundo, et totum mundum mihi soli.' " (God gave me alone to all the world, and all the world to me alone.) An example of the pointed style, as well as the thought, of Seneca is " Wants here may be seen and enjoyed; enjoyments there shall be seen, but wanted "(of Heaven and Hell).

This religious strain counted also upon the Continent; among certain sects, such as the Labadists of the seventeenth century, Seneca and Thomas à Kempis were held in high favor on account of their mystic qualities. We have a pretty picture of a young Dutch girl, Anna van Schurman,[24] whose father reads the philosophy of Seneca to her by way of initiation into Latin,— an interest which is reflected in many a " Life and Letters " of the period. Rubens and Vondel were fond of Seneca; and Grotius quotes from the 117th *Epistle,* with reference to the principle that consent is the basis of law.

Dryden, Langbaine, and Patrick Hannay in England hold Seneca in great secular respect. Dryden's maiden verses, on Lord Hastings, place him in great company:

" O *had he died of old, how great a strife*
  Had been who from his death should draw their
  life!

Who should, by one rich draught, become whate'er
Seneca, Cato, Numa, Caesar were,
Learned, virtuous, pious, great, and have by this
An universal metempsychosis!"

And Langbaine, in the essay on Dryden where he criticizes the drama *Indian Emperor,* remarks on plagiarisms " from Plutarch, Seneca, Montaigne, Fletcher," etc.

Hannay, in *A Happy Husband:*

" *Seneca saith, the gods did take delight*
To see grave Cato with his fate to fight."

Milton, in his treatise *On Education,* recommends the reading of the *Naturales Quaestiones,* although he seems not so reverent when he speaks of " Seneca, *in his books* a philosopher."

Finally, Fontenelle's *Dialogues des Morts* (1683) represents Scarron, author of the burlesque on the *Aeneid,* holding converse with Seneca on the proximity of the sublime to the ridiculous.

Up to this point Seneca has been called as a witness under favorable circumstances. We must now note a change in the spirit of the times. The eighteenth century paused to elaborate and take stock, after an adventurous sixteenth and a speculative seventeenth. Now Seneca is not an author whom anyone would regard as finished. The general reading public ran more towards vignettes of the past, or long treatises on small topics, or burlesque studies of serious themes. There was a narrower margin between the dignified and the absurd. People were not looking forward in the age of Queen Anne, nor was freshness or originality the watchword. The best spirits made fun of the world, and its pioneer newspapers waxed sarcastic. Rousseau was almost as unhappy in England as he was in France. Emotion and decorum had lost connection with one another. The critics became skeptical over the old masters. " I assure you, sir," says one,[25] " I shall, in the enjoyment of your letters, think myself little less honoured than I do Lucillius by Seneca's." Lord Shaftesbury had doubted Seneca's right to stand among the moral leaders of the world: " Few indeed (as the satirist says) are so detestable as to prefer Nero to Seneca; but how many would prefer Seneca to Rufus? For see how even Tacitus himself treats this latter." William Wotton (1666–1726), in his Essay on *Ancient and*

Modern Learning, declares: " That there is no such thing as a decay of eloquence in after ages, which have the performances of those that went before constantly to recur to, and which may be supposed to pretend to skill and fineness, is evident from the writings of Seneca and the younger Pliny, compared with Tully's."

France at this time began a systematic deprecation of Stoicism. Bossuet,[26] Fénelon and Pascal (who had received much benefit from it during their early training) compared Stoicism, to its own disadvantage, with the best type of Christianity, thereby undermining its ancillary value as an adjunct and an aid to Christian faith in the minds of intelligent contemporaries, both scholars and churchmen. La Bruyère and Malebranche laughed Stoicism away. The latter declared that Seneca resembled " ceux qui dansent, qui finissent toujours ou ils ont commencés "; and he maintained that the idea of putting the sage on a parity with the gods was futile: that Seneca's conception of the wise man was pompous, that the imagination of the Roman slipped its leash, and that continual droning about Cato was a bore. Malebranche did not understand, as Jeremy Taylor and Vaughan — saints both — had understood, that many a wondrous paradox would be weakened, including parts of the New Testament, if such a policy of filing and repression were continually employed. And we must remember that to Pascal the especial " pagans " were Epictetus and Montaigne. Elizabeth of Bohemia [27] had written to Descartes that she preferred his morality and his reasoning powers to Seneca's. After receiving from Descartes an account of the philosophy of Seneca, Epicurus, Zeno, and Aristotle, she replies: " I attribute the obscurity to be found in his book, as well as in most of the ancient writers, to a manner of explaining quite unlike ours, so that the same things which are problematical amongst us may pass for hypotheses with them, and the want of connection and order which he observes to the design of gaining admirers by astonishing the admiration, rather than disciples by informing the judgment; that Seneca uses fine phrases as others poetry or fable, to attract youth to follow his opinion." But none of these critics went so far as La Rochefoucauld, who makes Seneca the frontispiece to his *Maximes,* portrayed as a rascal with a mask of virtue.

On both sides of the English channel the
Age of Reason was tending to empiricism and
pragmatism. A French thinker could condemn
Stoicism as a " *jeu d'esprit* like Plato's Republic," and the so-called sage as a " fantôme
de vertu et de constance! " It is natural, and
we can understand even Bossuet — the Dau-
phin-guide, the writer of the Letter to Pope
Innocent, the ecclesiastical scholar, like Seneca
in so many ways — when he cries: " Laissez
vôtre Sénèque avec ses superbes opinions. Ce
philosophe insultait aux misères du genre hu-
main par une raillerie arrogante." Montes-
quieu revolts also: picturing a Persian travel-
ling in Europe and writing home from France
(as Goldsmith's Citizen of the World writes
home to China), Usbek says: " When a
European meets with misfortune, his only
resource is to read a philosopher called Seneca;
when an Asiatic falls into sorrow, he at least
has recourse to a stimulating beverage." The
eighteenth century, weary of enthusiasms, was
weary of Seneca also.

The course in England runs rather similarly
to that in France. Addison quotes the *sacer
intra nos spiritus,* which we have noted in
considering the congeniality between Seneca

and the early church. Bolingbroke's *Reflex-*
ions in Exile are like Seneca's own essay from
Corsica; but enthusiasm seems lacking. Goldsmith compares unfavorably the style of the
Italian composers with that of Seneca (in his
Schools of Music); Sir William Temple comments on the decline of the Latin tongue after
the time of Cicero; Watts (*Hero's School of
Morality*) sings a similar lullaby:

> " *Lie still, my Plutarch, then, and sleep,*
> *And you, good Seneca, may keep*
> *Your volumes closed forever, too;*
> *I have no further use for you;* "

and the Parson in *Tom Jones* bolsters two
harangues by burlesquing Seneca. There are,
however, two stout worthies who remain loyal.
Diderot,[28] who had disparaged Seneca in his
own essay *On Merit and Virtue*, took up the
cudgels later in life, became interested in La
Grange, the translator of Seneca, and fought
La Harpe on the question of the Roman philosopher's place in the history of morals. And
the last voice of the old school is raised in his
favor. Boswell declared: " For Seneca I have
a double reverence, both for his own worth,

and he was the heathen sage whom my grand-
father constantly studied."

Thus rationalizing France, and England,
which was preparing for Adam Smith and in-
dustrial invention, were not favorable ground
for a philosophy that depended for its head-
way upon a purely intellectual type of idealism. New things were coming; but only
two great masters of those days maintained
the view which put Seneca among the leaders
of thought: these were Rousseau and Voltaire.

Rousseau, who, says Diderot, " reminds us
of Seneca in a hundred ways," wrecked a
France still medieval. Essentially flexible in
his style and manner, Rousseau broke new
ground in his *Discourse on the Arts and Sci-
ences,* an essay which was published in 1750
and which embodies the fundamental principles of his creed. The glory of the country,
the grandeur of simplicity, the aspect of
virtue in its essentials: all these ideas fore-
stall the Rousseauism with which we are
familiar, and despite debate on the subject
of what is Classicism and what is Romanti-
cism, are the keynote to our ideas of the French
innovator. The " follow Nature " motto is
hard to define; but it certainly was not the

old order. Rousseau is also frank enough to criticize Seneca, and does not follow him slavishly.

Voltaire is always discriminating; he says in *Candide:* "There are bundles of sermons which all put together are not worth a single page of Seneca." How far Voltaire is in earnest here we cannot tell; for he also speaks of Calvin with tongue in cheek: "He knew some Latin, some Greek, and some of the bad philosophy current in his day." And Madame de Staël thought that Seneca's philosophy "penetrated farther into the heart of man" than Cicero's.

Macaulay and Niebuhr disagree with, and disapprove of, Seneca. Macaulay takes the side of Posidonius in regard to the topic discussed in the 90th *Epistle,* maintaining that the earlier inventors had a right to be called philosophers. Landor handles him roughly in the *Imaginary Conversations,* preferring Epictetus and a simple life lived without any advertisement of "honest poverty." He also hits at him in a portrait-skit:

"I *voted we should have but two*
At dinner; these are quite enow;

One of them, worth half Rome, will meet us,
Low-stationed, high-souled Epictetus.
He told his mind the other day
To ruby-fingered Seneca,
Who, rich and proud as Nero, teaches
The vanity of pomp or riches."

One doubts whether Epictetus would have sat down to dinner with Landor; Seneca could have handled him better in conversation. And when Landor accuses Seneca, in the mouth of Epictetus, of diverging " from the plain homely truths of Zeno and Cleanthes," it is hardly fair to hold Epictetus as the authority. Stoicism would never have grown into the great bulwark of practical Rome, if its votaries had not left Zeno and Cleanthes far behind.

Sydney Smith, an empiricist like most of his contemporaries, is a bit nettled also. On being left one-third of a fortune by his brother Courtenay, he writes: " After buying into the Consols and the Reduced, I read Seneca on *The Contempt of Wealth.* What intolerable nonsense! I have been happier every guinea I have gained." And, " The longer I live the more convinced I am that the apothecary is of more importance than Seneca."

Before the nineteenth century is well under way and before Seneca comes into his own again, there is some mixed evidence. Goethe recommends the *Naturales Quaestiones* as "charming" reading. Leigh Hunt refers to him. Charles Lamb proves the enduring name of the Roman by a remark on his use as a pedagogical medium: "Though they (mercenary schoolmasters) put into his (the scholar's) hands the fine sayings of Seneca and Epictetus, yet they themselves are none of those disinterested pedagogues to teach philosophy *gratis*." Coleridge is interesting in the variety of his criticism. He says in one place: "There is in some men an affected pride of spirit suitable only to the doctrine of the Stoics as it is usually taken." He mentions also "certain brilliant inconsistencies of Seneca"; but he quotes him on many occasions with approval, especially in one of his *Aphorisms:* "To those who decry the doctrine of the Spirit in man and its possible communion with the Holy Spirit as vulgar enthusiasm, I submit the following sentence from a pagan philosopher, a nobleman, and a minister of state; ' Ita dico, Lucili, sacer intra nos spiritus sedet.' "

The text to Wordsworth's *Ode to Duty* is

from Seneca. So is the patched-up motto " nil sapientiae odiosius acumine nimio," prefixed by Poe to his *Purloined Letter*. De Quincey quotes him and couples him with Sir Thomas Browne as a master of *rhetorica utens*. And Thomas Jefferson, writing to a favorite nephew, urges him to become familiar with Seneca, as well as with Epictetus, Plato, Xenophon, and Cicero.

But there are three literary critics of undoubted taste and authority who restore Seneca to his proper standing. These men understand that the question is not one of attempting to square statesmanship with philosophy, but how much of value Seneca contributes to the spirit and the intellect. Matthew Arnold calls him a stimulating writer; Sainte-Beuve declares, " La vraie baguette d'enchantment de Sénèque, c'est d'abord son style . . . le style, un sceptre d'or à qui reste, en définitive, l'empire de ce monde." Emerson,[29] especially in the recently published Journals, records of his workshop, shows again and again that he has read and pondered the ancient master with care. He records reading Montaigne to see how he approaches Seneca; he comes back often to the Stoic: " putting oneself into harmony with the constitution of things." Speaking of Burton and the "vocabulary class" of writers, he says: "Now and then out of that affluence of their learning comes a fine sentence from Theophrastus, Seneca, or Boethius, but no high method, no inspiring efflux." "Let us learn to live coarsely, dress plainly, and lie hard." "Sad is this continual postponement of life." Finally, the Journal of 1820–4 records Seneca as a regular part of the reading-course in ancient authors. There is much in common between the two,— their scorn of commitment to any one system, their open-mindedness, and their self-sufficiency and independence of doctrine. He cries out for calm, like Seneca and like the French quietist Joubert, who said: "aimer le repos, le repos," reminding us of the "retreat" of Seneca, the living within oneself. This, after all, is Seneca's greatest contribution to the thought of the world.

Nietzsche perhaps condemns himself by writing of him:

"*Seneca et hoc genus omne*
Das schreibt und schreibt sein unausstehlich weises harifari,
Als gaelt es primum scribere, deinde philosophari."

And Victor Hugo, in his loud impressiveness, cries:

> " *L'austère Sénèque, en louant Diogéne,*
>   *Buvait le Falerne dans l'or.*"

Herman Melville, writer of sea-tales, describing the costume of a frigate officer going into battle, thinks of the last days of the Roman: " No ill-will concerning his tailor should intrude upon his thoughts of eternity. Seneca understood this when he chose to die naked in a bath." Lord Coleridge takes Seneca away with him for vacation reading, along with Cowper, Cicero, Wordsworth, and Livingston.

Poets of recent date have turned to his proverbial sayings, as did Chaucer five hundred years before them. John Godfrey Saxe (*Compensation*) sings:

> " *When once, in Merrie England,*
>   *A prisoner of state*
>   *Stood waiting death or exile,*
>   *Submissive to his fate,*
>   *He made this famous answer,*—
>   ' *Si longa levis,*
>   *Dura, brevis,*
>   *Go and tell your tyrant chief!* ' "

[133]

And Richard Watson Dixon, in his poem on *St. Paul*, pictures Gallio as describing to his brother Seneca the famous meeting with the apostle. And who that was present, or heard the account from one who was present, could ever forget the tribute to Grover Cleveland, from the lips of James Russell Lowell at the Harvard Anniversary celebration of 1886? " He has left the helm of state, to be with us here, and so long as it is intrusted to his hands we are sure that, should the storm come, he will say with Seneca's Pilot: ' O Neptune, you may save me if you will; you may sink me if you will; but whatever happen, I shall keep my rudder true.' "

VIII. CONCLUSIONS

THE SCHOLARLY vote now puts Seneca where he belongs. Mr. Livingstone declares: " It is almost impossible to persuade those who do not know it, that classical literature is in any sense modern; they think of it as something primitive and barbarous, and they will not believe that Euripides or Seneca have as much in common with the twentieth century as Scott or Thackeray." And another modern educator, stressing the theory of imitation which underlies all the training of youth, turns to Seneca again for backing: " Long is the road through precepts, short and effective through examples." Dr. Osler, also, joins the throng of Senecans by echoing the famous passage, already quoted, on the joys of reading: " If you are fond of books, you will escape the ennui of life; you will neither sigh for evening, disgusted with the occupations of the day, nor will you live dissatisfied with yourself or unprofitable to others."

Maeterlinck rates Seneca high. He is re-

ported to have said, when asked what books he
should choose if he were limited to three only,
that one of these would be Pintrel's translation of the *Letters*. And it is interesting to
note that this book is to be reprinted in France
as a memorial on the tercentenary of the birth
of LaFontaine, to whom Pintrel had be-
queathed the manuscript and under whose aus-
pices it was published in 1684. In his *Essay on
Death,* Maeterlinck says: "If physicians thus
delay the end of a torture which, as good Seneca says, is the best part of that torture, they
are only yielding to the unanimous error which
daily strengthens the circle wherein it is con-
fined."

Seneca will soon come into his own. There
is now a period of freer thought and of deeper
religion on the way. The elasticity in literature which, though crude, betokens an era of
progress; the possibility of raising the conscience of a nation to the standards of an
individual; and the philosophy of freedom
from fettered prejudices,— all these phenom-
ena are of a sort with which the subject of this
sketch would have readily sympathized.
Eucken was right when he penned these words:
" In the period of the Enlightenment the writ-

ings of a Lucretius and a Seneca, a Plutarch and a Marcus Aurelius, were in the hands of all cultivated persons. Since the rise of modern Humanism, however, this is no longer the case. But do not the more vigorous development of the individual and the intensifying of life which we are experiencing to-day bring us nearer again to later antiquity? "

We have seen that in periods when new ideas are in the air, Seneca furnishes material for the promoter and for the interpreter of progress. We noted his influence as a forerunner or an *ex post facto* advocate of the Christian religion. Montaigne, in breaking up the artificialities of a worn-out chivalry in France, draws from the Corduban as from a never-failing spring. Petrarch's return to the classics signalized itself by close adaptation to the style of Seneca. Chaucer's English leadership, Elizabethan pioneering, the experiments of Rousseau, and the various attempts to explain philosopher-kingship during the last eight centuries — all these are indicative of a latent power which has never been sufficiently acknowledged.

One is led to speculate whether, as the modern materialistic tendency declines and the power of mind and spirit increases, the originality of Seneca's message may not again be an auxiliary force in the world's progress toward a deeper Christianity.

NOTES AND BIBLIOGRAPHY

NOTES

Limitation of space imposed by the plan of this series forbids the inclusion of complete references which would be expected in a longer work. Therefore only the most essential notes of a general nature are given, but the author will gladly furnish further references to interested scholars.

1. Horace, *Odes*, III. 6. 31 f.
      navis Hispanae magister,
      dedecorum pretiosus emptor.

2. Martial, IV. 40. 2, *i.e.*, the Elder Seneca, Seneca the Younger (our philosopher), and Lucan, the former's grandson. Cf. also VII. 45. 1. (*facundus Seneca*), I. 61. 7 ff., and XII. 36. 8 ff.

3. Cf. Epigram 8 (of doubtful authenticity), *Ad Helv.* (ed. Duff) 2. 5; 18. 4–6, etc.

4. James Boswell, *An Account of Corsica*, London, 1768.

5. Tacitus, *Ann.* 15. 61 ff., trans. Ramsay.

6. A summary of the most important testimony regarding Seneca may be found as follows: Pliny, *N.H.*, 14. 4; 14. 51. Columella, *R. R.*, 3. 3. Juvenal, 5. 109, etc. Ausonius, p. 361 (ed. Peiper). Fronto (ed. Naber) pp. 123, 155–8, 224. Quintilian, 10. 1. 125. Gellius, *Noct. Att.*, 12. 2. 2 ff. Plutarch, *Moral.*, 3. 201 and *Galba*, 20. Boethius, *Cons. Phil.*, 1 Pref. 3. Macrobius, *Sat.*, 1. 11. 7 ff. A complete story is found in Tacitus, *Ann.* 12. 8; 13. 2, 5 ff., 25, 28 ff., 42; 14. 52 ff.; 15. 45, 60 ff. Cf. also Dio, 59. 19; 61. 3–4, etc.; and Suetonius, *Calig.*, *Claud.*, and *Nero*. Suetonius is now accessible in the *Loeb Library*, translated by J. C. Rolfe; Dio, in the same series, by E. Cary, is forthcoming.

7. Pliny, *Nat. Hist.*, 9. 53; 6 and 36.

[141]

8. Cf. A. S. Pease, "The Attitude of Jerome towards Pagan Literature," in *Transactions of the American Philological Association*, L. 150–167 (1919).

9. Trans. W. H. Porter, in E. Vernon Arnold's *Roman Stoicism*, Cambridge, 1911, pp. 86 ff.

10. Sen., *Brev. Vit.*, 14. 2. *V. B.*, 13. 1. *Ep.*, 2. 5; 85. 1; 88. 44; 108. 22. For the whole subject of soul and body in Seneca, cf. *Ep.* 24. 18; 65. 24; *Ad Polyb.*, 5. 1 and 9. 2, (statement of the problem). *Ep.* 54. 4, 71. 15, 82. 15 ff., and Frag. 28, (negation). *Ep.* 36. 9 ff., 75. 17 ff., 63. 16, 92. 30 ff., 102. 1 and 22 ff., and *Helv.* 11. 6 ff., (approval of immortality).

11. *Quid de Deo Seneca Senserit*, Paris, 1884; E. Westerburg, *Der Ursprung der Sage dass Seneca Christ gewesen sei*, Berlin, 1881. Min. Fel., *Octav.*, 33. 1; Tertul., *De Anima*, 20; Lact., *Inst.*, 1. 5; Sen., *Ep.* 8. 7, 41. 2, 92. 30.

12. For the modern tendencies discussed in the preceding pages, the author has made frequent use of his "Modern Note in Seneca's Letters," in *Classical Philology*, X. 139–150 (1915). For a beginning of the studies to which the rest of this book is devoted, see *Proceedings of the American Philological Association*, XLII. 38–40 (1911), and XLIII. 26–29 (1912). W. C. Summers, *Selected Letters of Seneca*, London, 1910; Introduction, Section C, contains much valuable material.

13. *Ad Paul. de Brev. Vit.*, 14 f.

14. Cf. J. E. B. Mayor, "Seneca in Alain of Lille," in *Journal of Philology*, XX. 1–6 (1892).; A. de I., trans. by D. M. Moffat, New York, 1908 (Holt), esp. pp. 34, 58, 67, 73, 91.

15. V. of B., Bk. 4, ch. 70; Bk. 6., ch. 38. Girald., Everyman edn., p. 151, etc. J. S. Brewer, *Life of Bacon*, p. 73, in *Works of Roger Bacon*, London, 1859. J. E. Sandys, *A History of Classical Scholarship*, Cambridge, 1908; I. 569, 574.

16. *Metalogicus*, 1. 22. *Policraticus*, 5. 10 and 8. 13. *Contra Jov.* ch. 48.

17. F. S. Stevenson, *Life of G.*, London, 1899, pp. 34 ff., 91 ff.; H. R. Luard's edn. of G.'s *Letters*, London, 1861.

18. Cf. E. Moore, *Studies in Dante*, Oxford, 1896 —,

1st Ser., pp. 14, 16, 198, 288 ff. P. Toynbee, *Dante Stud. and Res.*, New York, 1902, pp. 40 and 150 ff. *Inferno*, 4. 141; *Convito*, 1. 8, 2. 14, 4. 12, 14. 12, and *Ep.* 4. 5. These may be compared with Sen. *Ep.*, 95. 3, 76; 109. 17 ff.; *N. Q.*, 1. 1, 7. 17, etc.

19. Cf. an excellent monograph by Harry M. Ayres, "Chaucer and Seneca," in *Romanic Review*, X. 1–15 (1919). See also T. R. Lounsbury, *Chaucer Studies*, New York, 1902; II. 249 ff.

20. Cf. De Nolhac, *Petrarch et l'Humanisme*, Paris, 1907; Petrarch, *Letters to Classical Authors*, trans. M. E. Cosenza, New York, 1898, esp. pp. 88 ff.; J. H. Robinson and H. W. Rolfe, *Petrarch*, Chicago, 1910; Int., p. 50, pp. 141, 151 ff., 230 ff., 281.

21. Cf. P. Villey, *Les Sources et l'Évolution des Essais de Montaigne*, Paris, 1908; esp. I. 15 ff., 99, and 279. Also, A. A. Tilley, *Lit. Fr. Renaiss.*, Cambridge, 1904; I. 303 and II. 254, etc. Compare with Seneca, Montaigne's *De la Modération*, *De la Colère*, *Du Jeune Caton*, *Des Livres*, *De la Gloire*, etc.

22. Cf. J. E. Spingarn, *Critical Essays of the 17th Century*, Oxford, 1909; I. Int., 15, 36, 52, etc. F. E. Schelling, *Jonson's Timber*, Boston, 1892, *passim*. For Shakespeare, cf. E. A. Sonnenschein, "Latin as an Intellectual Force in Civilization," in *National Review*, XLVII. 670–683 (1906); Sir S. Lee, *Shakespeare and the Modern Stage*, New York, 1906, pp. 152 ff.

23. Cf. J. Spedding, *Works of B.*, *passim*, esp. 6. 274 and 7. 120. E. G. Bourne, *Seneca and the Discovery of America*, New York, 1901. I. B. Richman, *The Spanish Conquerors*, New Haven, 1919, p. 17.

24. Cf. Una Birch, *Life of Anna van Schurman*, London, 1909, pp. 16n., 72, 167.

25. Forde, *Familiar Letters*, ed. A. H. Upham, *French Influence in English Literature*, New York, 1908, p. 445.

26. Malebranche, *Tr. de Morale*, and *Rech. de la Vérité*, 1. 17. 3; 2. 3. 4; 4. 10; 5. 2 and 4. La Bruyère, *De l'Homme*, 2. 3 ff. Fénelon, *Examen de Conscience*. Pascal, *Thoughts*, ed. Wight, Boston, 1884; 8. 13; 2. 13. Bossuet, *Tr. de la*

Concup.; *Sur la Loi de Dieu*; etc. Cf. H. L. Lear, *Bossuet and his Contemporaries*, New York, 1875, p. 103.

27. E. Godfrey, *A Sister of Prince Rupert*. pp. 170 ff.

28. John Morley, *Diderot*, London, 1891; 2. 232 ff.

29. Cf. Dartmouth Address; *Journals*, 4. 78, etc.; *Books* (Fireside edn., 7. 201); Essay on Prudence, — "Lite wastes itself while we are beginning to live," from Sen. *Ep.* 1; and many other echoes. See also *Journals*, 1820–4, p. 203; 1833–5, p. 539; and 1836–8, p. 406.

BIBLIOGRAPHY

BOUCHIER, E. S., *Spain under the Roman Empire*. Oxford, 1914.

CLARKE, J., and GEIKIE, SIR ARCHIBALD, *Physical Science in the Time of Nero* (Being a Translation of the *Quaestiones Naturales* of Seneca). London, 1910.

FRANK, T., *Economic History of Rome*. New York, 1920.

GUMMERE, R. M., *Seneca Ad Lucilium Epistulae Morales, with an English Translation*, in *The Loeb Classical Library*. New York, 1917 and 1920. (vols. I and II, ready; with bibliography).

LODGE, THOMAS, *Translation of Seneca's prose works*. London, 1614.

PICHON, R., "Un Philosophe Ministre sous l'Empire Romain," in *Revue des Deux Mondes*, LIX. 363–394 (1910).

WALTZ, RENÉ, *Vie de Sénèque*. Paris, 1909 (with bibliography).

Those interested in the Tragedies of Seneca, which this volume does not aim to discuss, may consult: Miller, F. J., *The Tragedies of Seneca* (translated into English Verse). Chicago, 1907; *Seneca's Tragedies, with an English Translation*, in *The Loeb Classical Library*. 2 vols. New York, 1917. Cunliffe, J. W., *The Influence of Seneca on Elizabethan Tragedy*. Manchester, 1893. It is assumed that the Tragedies are genuine; it has even been held by Pease, A. S., "Is the *Octavia* a Play of Seneca?", in *Classical Journal*, XV. 388–403 (1920), that the *Octavia*, that melancholy drama of Nero's first wife, comes from the same pen, — an experiment in contemporary portrayal which was rare upon the ancient stage. Cf., besides Cunliffe, *op. cit.*, Lucas, F. L., *Seneca and Elizabethan Tragedy*. Cambridge University Press, 1922; Thorndike, A. H., *Tragedy*. Boston, 1908; pp. 33–75; and Schelling, F. E., *Elizabethan Drama*. Boston, 1908; I. 87 ff., II. 2 ff.

Our Debt to Greece and Rome

AUTHORS AND TITLES

AUTHORS AND TITLES

HOMER. *John A. Scott.*

SAPPHO. *David M. Robinson.*

EURIPIDES. *F. L. Lucas.*

ARISTOPHANES. *Louis E. Lord.*

DEMOSTHENES. *Charles D. Adams.*

THE POETICS OF ARISTOTLE. *Lane Cooper.*

GREEK RHETORIC AND LITERARY CRITICISM. *W. Rhys Roberts.*

LUCIAN. *Francis G. Allinson.*

CICERO AND HIS INFLUENCE. *John C. Rolfe.*

CATULLUS. *Karl P. Harrington.*

LUCRETIUS AND HIS INFLUENCE. *George Depue Hadzsits.*

OVID. *Edward Kennard Rand.*

HORACE. *Grant Showerman.*

VIRGIL. *John William Mackail.*

SENECA THE PHILOSOPHER. *Richard Mott Gummere.*

APULEIUS. *Elizabeth Hazelton Haight.*

MARTIAL. *Paul Nixon.*

PLATONISM. *Alfred Edward Taylor.*

ARISTOTELIANISM. *John L. Stocks.*

STOICISM. *Robert Mark Wenley.*

LANGUAGE AND PHILOLOGY. *Roland G. Kent.*

AUTHORS AND TITLES

AESCHYLUS AND SOPHOCLES. *J. T. Sheppard.*

GREEK RELIGION. *Walter Woodburn Hyde.*

SURVIVALS OF ROMAN RELIGION. *Gordon J. Laing.*

MYTHOLOGY. *Jane Ellen Harrison.*

ANCIENT BELIEFS IN THE IMMORTALITY OF THE SOUL. *Clifford H. Moore.*

STAGE ANTIQUITIES. *James Turney Allen.*

PLAUTUS AND TERENCE. *Gilbert Norwood.*

ROMAN POLITICS. *Frank Frost Abbott.*

PSYCHOLOGY, ANCIENT AND MODERN. *G. S. Brett.*

ANCIENT AND MODERN ROME. *Rodolfo Lanciani.*

WARFARE BY LAND AND SEA. *Eugene S. McCartney.*

THE GREEK FATHERS. *James Marshall Campbell.*

GREEK BIOLOGY AND MEDICINE. *Henry Osborn Taylor.*

MATHEMATICS. *David Eugene Smith.*

LOVE OF NATURE AMONG THE GREEKS AND ROMANS. *H. R. Fairclough.*

ANCIENT WRITING AND ITS INFLUENCE. *B. L. Ullman.*

GREEK ART. *Arthur F. irbanks.*

ARCHITECTURE. *Alfred M. Brooks.*

ENGINEERING. *Alexander P. Gest.*

MODERN TRAITS IN OLD GREEK LIFE. *Charles Burton Gulick.*

ROMAN PRIVATE LIFE. *Walton Brooks McDaniel.*

GREEK AND ROMAN FOLKLORE. *William Reginald Halliday.*

ANCIENT EDUCATION. *J. F. Dobson.*